DREAM SH

DREAM
SHARING

A Guide to Understanding Dreams by Sharing and Discussion

ROBIN SHOHET

First published by Turnstone Press
1985
This edition 1989

British Library Cataloguing in
Publication Data

Shohet, Robin
Dream sharing: a guide to
understanding dreams by sharing and
discussion.
1. Dreams. Interpretation
I. Title
154.6'34

ISBN 1-85274-058-2

*Crucible is an imprint of The Aquarian
Press, part of the Thorsons Publishing
Group, Wellingborough,
Northamptonshire, NN8 2RQ, England*

Printed and bound in Great Britain by
Mackays of Chatham PLC, Chatham, Kent

3   5   7   9   10   8   6   4   2

To my father, Joan, and Sam,
with love.

ACKNOWLEDGEMENTS

I would first like to thank members of my original peer dream group – Brenda Goldstein, Andrew Forrester, Judy Ryde and my partner Joan Wilmot. It was writing about that group that led to the book. Next come all the people who have so willingly shared their dreams with me, especially those who have given me permission to describe their work in detail. I would particularly like to thank those of them who contributed their accounts of our work together for the book – namely Teri Connolly, Jane Read, Sandy Kondos, Andy McGeeney and Margaret Toback.

My thanks are also due to Ann and Alick Bartholomew for starting me on the project. At the beginning when I went to America to gather ideas, Jeremy Taylor, John van Damm, Meredith Sabini, Strephon Williams and Dick McLeester were all extremely helpful and willing to make resources available. On my return Ian Gordon Brown supported me through my initial doubts, and Margaret Caffrey provided a place for me to write. Later John Heron lovingly confronted me as I struggled and helped me overcome some of my writing blocks. About that time Tony Crisp provided me with many useful suggestions which I have incorporated into the book.

Brian Wade has been a continual source of information on books on dreams and related topics. Peter Hawkins Julian Brown and Sarah Buxton have been good friends throughout the time of writing and I have valued their goodwill. In the later stages Vin Gomez spent many hours going through the manuscript with me and I appreciate the care she took. To Mel and Ena Demetriades I owe a lot. Without their outstanding generosity in providing me with a flat when I needed to be totally alone for the final stages, the work might not have come to fruition.

I have been influenced by many people's ideas on dreams. However Winifred Rushforth who was running dream groups until just before she died in her ninety-ninth year, has been a particularly important figure for me.

Finally I would like to thank members of my immediate family – Joan, Ben and Joe for their patience, especially in the later stages when I was so absent from home. To Joan in particular I would like to express my love and thanks for co-facilitating dream groups with me and for helping me rewrite many parts of the book.

Contents

1.

ATTITUDES
TO DREAMS

I have been interested in dreams for over twenty years now – ever since waking from a nightmare in which Peter the Great, a tyrannical seventeenth-century Russian king, chased me into a toilet where I was able to use only two sheets of paper. I interpreted the dream immediately on waking as meaning that I would only pass two 'A' levels and fail my history examination, which I duly did. It was pretty obvious that I would fail anyway, so I did not see my dream as 'prophetic', but I enjoyed my interpretation and it impressed my girlfriend. I had also been reading Freud at the time, and realized that Peter the Great stood for some aspect of my relationship with my father. I was able to talk about the dream to him and for some time our relationship improved. I was thus not only able to interpret the dream, but share it in a very useful way.

These two aspects of dreamwork – meaning and sharing – have always gone side by side for me, and I have found that each can help the other. In this case the sharing enhanced the meaning as I became less afraid of my father. Very often the meaning of a dream only emerges when the dream is shared.

Dream interpretation has a long history. There is a Treatise on Dreams in one of the Indian Vedas which dates between the fifteenth and tenth century BC and includes long lists of favourable and unfavourable dreams. Dreams were an important part of life in ancient Egypt and Babylon, and the Bible contains many references to dreams. Most famous, perhaps, are Joseph's dreams where he foresees his relationship to his brothers and successfully interprets Pharoah's cattle dream, thereby helping to save Egypt from a potentially disastrous drought. The New Testament, however, contains no less than five dream warnings in the first two pages. And if each one had not been listened to, and acted upon, the whole course of religious history for the following two thousand years could have been basically altered. As Alan McGlashan says in *Gravity and Levity*,[1] 'Whether these stories are fact or fable is of little importance . . . Either way they attest the value given to the dreaming mind in those days as a guide to the immediate problems of life'.

Looking further afield, a number of so-called primitive tribes ascribe great importance to dreams and dream sharing in their daily lives, using them to help with decision making and maintenance of the community. Jung says, 'Primitives tell each other impressive dreams, in a public palaver if possible and this custom is also attested to in late antiquity for all ancient peoples attributed great significance to dreams'. In fact, looking at different cultures at different stages of history reveals how attitudes to dreams affect what is done with them. Thus dreams have been seen as nonsense, products of indigestion, the work of the devil, a message from God, communication with the dead, a form of prediction, wanderings of the soul and products of our unconscious, to name but a few. Each viewpoint will affect the dreamer's view of the dream and how he shares it, and the role and importance given to the official dream interpreter.

Our own view in the twentieth-century Western world has probably been affected by the decline in importance given to the dream by the Church, which chose to deal with dreams in terms of its confusion as to whether they came from God or the Devil, as opposed to looking for interpretations. In this way little active encouragement for working with dreams was given and the main sources of guidance were potted dream dictionaries, the like of which we still see today. The publication of Freud's *Interpretation of Dreams* in 1899 has had a profound influence not only on dream interpretation, but also on how dreams have been linked with a specialist to whom you go for treatment. There is also a strong body of opinion that sees dreams as meaningless and irrelevant to practical living. This viewpoint sees interest in them as self-indulgent, super-stitious and unscientific and denies the possibility that they may have something to say.

Between the so-called hard-headed rationalist and the psychoanalytic dream expert, I think a third position has begun to emerge in the last few years. There have been a spate of radio programmes on dreams, including 'phone-ins' for people's dreams. The *Daily Mail* started a dream column where hundreds of dreams were received, and from my work with dreams I have heard of dozens of people involved in self-help dream groups. However this only represents a very small percentage of the population and for the most part interest in dreams is still seen as a fringe subject and study of them is not likely to be seen, for example, on a school timetable.

I would invite you here to look at some of your attitudes to dreams and where you think they may have come from. A good way to do this is to write the word 'dreams' in the middle of a clean sheet of paper (I have included a diagram on the previous page which you can use) and draw lines from it like spokes from a wheel. Then write down your various attitudes to dreams at the end of each spoke. The idea is always to go back to the word 'dreams' in the middle before going on to the next association. I include my words below, but suggest you try yours before reading mine. The advantage of writing it as opposed to doing it verbally is that you will have a record and will be able to see if your words change with time.

How was it for you? Did the words reveal any connections you had not made before? Was the exercise interesting or did you just skip it? Does what you wrote tell you anything about why you are reading this book?

My words included Freud, sharing, unconscious, higher self, lower self, interpretation, intriguing, boring, revealing, honest, irrelevant and indulgent. You can see my enthusiasm for dreams does not protect me from a certain ambivalence, especially at the moment when I am putting so much energy into writing about them. I sometimes wonder, however, if I have been affected by our present culture more than I would like to think, and that in spite of having worked successfully with people's dreams, still feel a need to justify myself. While I was writing about our culture's attitudes to dreams, I mentioned the scientific-rational, the analytic-expert, and the more recent popular exponent who does not believe that the dream is meaningless or that it belongs in the province of the expert. I wondered about another category, the one which glorifies dreams and tells how you can change your life through dreams. These views, often American imports, promise a bigger, better self and although useful in correcting a cultural disregard for dreams, oversimplify and have a slight conversion feel to them. I hope that I will be able to show that dreams can be interesting and relevant to your life without implying that life without them cannot exist. For me it is not the dreams, but the sharing of them that has made them important in my life and that is why I have chosen to write about this area.

In my work as a therapist, I often use analogies with food

to show how people approach certain aspects of their life. Thus we talk of not being able to stomach something, it being too much to take in, digest or swallow. Dreaming alone, for me, is like eating alone. Both eating and dreaming are necessary (I shall present the evidence to show we all dream every night and that when deprived of dream sleep our mental balance can be affected), but it is the rituals around sharing that make the process meaningful. This social aspect is much neglected in dreamwork, with more interest being given to interpretation; but even here the social side cannot be ignored for it is well known that patients in Freudian analysis have Freudian dreams, and those in Jungian analysis have Jungian dreams and so on. In the one-to-one situation, there is a social context with the patient perhaps trying to please the analyst, or at least being affected by him or her.

On page 12 I quoted Jung, who talked of sharing dreams in a public palaver. I would very much like to see this happen more often. We are a society of mass media – it has never been easier to reach so many people, via satelite communication, television, radio, newspapers, and so on, but that can easily mislead us into thinking we are in contact with ourselves and other people. In fact, the media contact can be a substitute for real contact, and my desire to write a book about dream *sharing* and the recent popular interest in dreams may have a common element of people wanting to share and find out about themselves on a deeper level. Although I have been glad that there have been radio and television programmes on dreams, as well as increased coverage in newspapers, I am saddened that people have had to take their dreams to a total stranger. Some of the letters I have seen have been very moving, quoting dreams from many years back which have left a deep impression on the dreamer. My hope is that dream sharing can be introduced in such places as schools, day centres, the Church and hospitals, where dreams can be discussed with other people.

In suggesting this, I am aware that I may be crossing cultural norms which see dreams as private. Another cultural defence which ignores the common level of humanity we share in our dreams is the idea that 'There is nothing so boring as someone else's dream'. This fear of boring or revealing too much of oneself is easily overcome when regular sharing develops. For the meantime you might like to think of a time when you told someone a dream. What was their response? Did you get what you were looking for? Were you and the other person embarrassed, passing it off as 'only a dream'? Think of a time when someone told you a dream. What was your response?

My own experience is that since it has been known that I am writing a book on dreams, people from all walks of life have come up to me to ask me for interpretations. Most surprising and rewarding has been the response of my relatives. I was brought up in a very materialistic Iraqui Jewish culture where money confers very high status along with such professions as doctor, lawyer and accountant. However, the community has somehow been intrigued by my work on dreams. Relatives and even people I hardly know have telephoned to ask for interpretations. It is as if the irrational part of themselves, so denied by such emphasis on external status, has been given permission to emerge. I suspect they are not the only ones.

2.

NOT ONLY A DREAM

'As we grow older we gradually lose the ability to be surprised. This attitude is perhaps one reason why one of the most puzzling phenomena in our lives – our dreams – gives so little cause for wonder and for raising questions.'

Erich Fromm in The Forgotten Language[1]

'The dreaming mind, I suggest, in addition to all its other functions is an instrument of liberation, capable of breaking up the conventional patterns of human perception, and releasing new forms of awareness. I invite you to regard the dreaming mind as a *file* smuggled into a space-time cell where man lies captive; a cell whose walls and ceilings are our five senses, and whose warders are the inflexible concepts of logic.'

Alan McGlashan in The Savage and Beautiful Country.[2]

In the first chapter I briefly looked at a variety of attitudes to dreams through the ages, ranging from seeing them as meaningless to seeing them as messages from God. Modern advocates of the dream quote numerous examples of discoveries made during dreams over the last few centuries to show the creative power of dreams. These include the discovery of the molecular structure of benzine which revolutionized modern chemistry, the Theory of Relativity, the invention of the sewing machine. What these examples often omit is that their inventors had been heavily involved in working on their projects beforehand, and the dream was the final touch to a long process. I include the dreams themselves because I think they show how it is possible for dreams to transcend space-time boundaries and because I like them. (I am indebted to Jeremy Taylor and his book *Dream Work*[3] for these examples.)

Elias Howe invented the sewing machine after a dream in which he was captured by cannibals and tossed into a huge pot of water to cook alive. As the water began to bubble around him, his bonds loosened and he was able to free his hands, but each time he tried to climb out of the pot, the natives would poke him back with their spears. On awakening he realized that the spears had holes in the *points* and this led to the invention of the sewing machine, a project he had been working on, in vain, for some time.

One of the most world-changing ideas -- the Theory of Relativity – had a similar source. When asked when and where the idea for the theory first occurred to him, Albert Einstein quoted a dream which he had had in adolescence. In this dream he was riding on a sledge. As the sledge accelerated, going faster and faster until it approached the speed of light, the stars began to distort into amazing patterns and colours, dazzling him with the beauty and power of their transformation. He said that in many ways, his entire scientific career could be seen as an extended meditation on that dream.

My last example is Fredrich Kekule who had been trying for years to define the molecular structure of benzine. The answer came as he slept in a chair one afternoon. In his dream he saw a snake with its tail in its mouth. From this he realized benzine was a closed ring of carbon molecules. He was so taken by the nature of his discovery that at a research conference he urged his colleagues 'Gentlemen, learn to dream'.

Although many more examples could be given, they would not be typical of the average dreams that most of us have every night. In fact many people who start dreamwork with me either say they never dream or rarely remember their dreams. In the last few decades, however, the study of sleep has become scientifically respectable, and there is now overwhelming evidence that most of us dream four to five times a night.

This discovery was made in 1953 in the Department of Physiology at the University of Chicago, where research was being done on sleep under the guidance of Professor Kleitman. One of his students, Eugine Aserinsky, noticed that an infant's eyes moved rapidly and jerkily under the closed lids for short periods during sleep. He and Kleitman decided to see if this were true for adults too, by means of a machine called an electroencephalograph, which makes recordings of electrical impulses in the brain. It magnifies these impulses and translates them into a written record. In a similar way, electrodes placed round the eye will monitor eye movements during the night.

Through these records they discovered that there are four stages of sleep ranging from stage one, which is the lightest, to stage four which is the deepest. In a typical cycle a sleeper was seen to descend into deep sleep and then ascend to lighter sleep periodically in cycles lasting approximately ninety minutes. As the night went on, less time was spent in stages three and four and more in one or two. However, what is relevant to us is that when looking at the eye movement record they found that stages two, three and four were normally accompanied by no eye movements, or slow ones. Stage one, on the other hand, was accompanied by Rapid Eye Movements (REMs) as though the sleeper were watching some kind of scenario. There were other activities in REM sleep such as higher rate of oxygen consumption in the brain and irregularities in pulse and respiration rates and in blood-pressure. The researchers guessed that during REM sleep people were dreaming, as if they were watching a show. On waking them the researchers found that in eighty per cent of the cases the person could remember dreaming. It became possible to answer how often we dream, how long a dream lasts, and whether there are people who never dream. It was discovered that we dream on average five times a night, which amounts to well over a thousand dreams a year. The dreams become progressively longer as the night goes on; the first being about ten minutes and the last one before waking lasting up to forty-five minutes. On average the total dreaming time in a night's sleep is about ninety minutes.

Experiments were later carried out in which subjects were awoken from REM sleep but allowed to sleep at other times. It was hoped thereby to allow people to sleep but deprive them of dreams. What happened was the experiments became impossible to continue as the subjects fell back immediately into REM sleep when left to go back to sleep. On recovery nights, when they were allowed to sleep undisturbed, they spent up to twice as much time as normal in dream sleep. A control group which was awoken in non-REM periods reported no increase in dream sleep when left undisturbed. It seemed as if there might be a biological need to dream.

In 1959 a well-known disc jockey called Peter Tripp decided to stay awake for 200 hours to raise money for charity. Although his health remained good throughout, after two days he began to hallucinate and became progressively more psychotic as the experiment continued. His world became a waking nightmare. This again pointed to the need for sleep and dreams, as once the experiment ended he quite quickly returned to normal.

Despite these experiments, which are now well established, people still say frequently, 'I never dream'. If, as the research suggests, we have over 1,500 dreams a year, why do we not remember more of them? There are many possible reasons. Psychological tests have shown that it is personality characteristics rather than depth of sleep which distinguishes non-recallers from recallers. The former tend to be more inhibited, more conformist and more self-controlled on the whole, than recallers, who tend to be more overtly anxious about life and more willing to admit to common emotional disturbances, such as anxiety and insecurity. (My source here is Ann Faraday's excellent book *Dream Power*[1] where she examines the question of forgetting dreams in great detail. She also mentions Jung's two famous character types – extroverts and introverts – the former more concerned with their relationship to the external world and the latter their inner world, which might have some bearing on interest in dreams.)

Another possible reason which might have some overlap with personality type is that we all repress our dreams to some extent because they contain distressing ideas and wishes. This basically Freudian idea has some validity, and Ann Faraday describes how this resistance can even carry over to the sleep laboratory. For my part, I have observed that at the start of a dream group even a person who usually recalls their dreams begins to forget. It is as if they are testing out the water. Is it safe to tell a dream here? When they finally do remember a dream they usually agree that they had previously felt some restraint.

Part of the reason may be physiological – the difficulty of recalling dreams from the REM period. For example, if a subject is woken from a REM period he nearly always reports a vivid dream. If he is awakened five minutes after the end of a REM period, he will probably catch only fragments of it; and after ten minutes the dream is almost completely lost. Incidentally, I often tell the college students I teach that if they wake up in the middle of the night with a dream, no matter how many times they repeat it to themselves verbally, the chances are they will lose it unless they write it down. It seems that non-REM sleep can wipe out memory traces no matter how motivated you are.

However, I believe that the main reason why we do not remember our dreams more often than we do is that we have no cultural reinforcement to do so. In societies where dreams are shared each day, there is plenty of social reinforcement to remember and a particular type of dream might confer high status on the dreamer. This lack of social reinforcement even extends to the language of the dream. Our waking language and time structure do not correspond to the time distortions in dreams, or the apparent contradictions – it was my friend I saw but at the same time it wasn't. We have no ready way of translating the images into everyday language. It is for this reason I encourage group members to paint, dance, act out or write a poem of a dream. In this way a mood can be captured which would elude normal language. Our society does not offer help in bringing back the dream to everyday life and its indifference is, if anything, seen as proof of the meaninglessness of dreams. This point is taken up by Erich Fromm in his book *The Forgotten Language* and I quote from him at length. In commenting on our everyday attitudes he says,

> When we are awake, we are active, rational beings, eager to make an effort to get what we want.and prepared to defend ourselves against attack. We act and we observe; we see things outside, perhaps not as they are, but at least in such a manner that we can use and manipulate them . . . We call this field of our day-time observation 'reality' and are proud of our 'realism' and our cleverness in manipulating it.[5]

As we know well dreams do not follow such laws of logic and are not so accessible to manipulation. Moreover it is not only outside events that are different but we ourselves. As Fromm says,

> The paradoxical fact is that we are not only less reasonable and less decent in our dreams, but we are also more intelligent, wiser and capable of better judgement when we are asleep than when we are awake.[6]

Fromm compares the language of sleep and dreams to those of myth and says,

> The dreams of ancient and modern man are written in the same language as the myths whose authors lived in the dawn of history. This symbolic language is a language in which inner experiences, feelings and thoughts are expressed as if they were sensory experiences, events in the outer world. It is a language which has a different logic from the conventional one we speak in the daytime, a logic in which not time and space are the ruling categories but intensity and association . . . Yet this language has been forgotten by modern man. Not when he is asleep, but when he is awake. Is it not important to understand this language also in our waking state?[7]

Fromm answers his own question,

> For the people of the past, living in the great culture of both East and West, there was no doubt as to the answer to this question. For them myths and dreams were among the most

significant expressions of the mind. It is only in the past few hundred years of Western culture that this attitude has changed. At best, myths were supposed to be naïve fabrications of the pre-scientific mind, created long before man had made his great discoveries about nature and had learned some of the secrets of its mastery. Dreams fared worse and were considered plain senseless and unworthy of attention. If they had been pleasant it might have been that they would have been met with more friendliness. But many of them leave us in an anxious mood; often they are nightmares from which we awake grateful that it was only a dream. Others although not nightmares are disturbing for other reasons. They do not fit the person we are sure we are during the daytime. We dream of hating the person we are fond of and loving someone who we thought did not interest us. We dream of being ambitious when we are convinced of being modest, of being terrified when we think we are brave. But worse than all this is the fact that we do not understand our dreams, while we, the waking person are sure we can understand anything if we put our minds to it. Rather than be confronted with such an over-whelming proof of the limitations of our understanding, we accuse the dreams of not making sense.[8]

Having dwelt at great length on some of the cultural reasons for forgetting dreams, I do not want to leave the responsibility there. Although I have no difficulty in remembering my dreams, I often still ignore the messages they might be offering. Here is a personal example. Some time ago, I was considering living in a community, joining a group, some of whom were friends, some strangers. Whilst in the middle of negotiating for a place, I had a dream about one of the members of the group. In the dream my flat was being attacked by vandals, and I managed to escape to her house down the road. She was having a party and wasn't the slightest bit interested in helping. It wasn't only the content, but the feeling of indifference which was a warning sign to me. Nevertheless I continued going to meetings because consciously I believed that the group and this woman in particular were very committed. Had I been willing to listen to my dream, or even better, share it, I think it would have been of benefit to all concerned as the group did later fold up.

Erich Fromm gives an excellent example of the same process of refusing to allow into consciousness impressions which appear very clearly formed in dreams. He tells of a man who, the day before, had been to meet someone who was considered a 'very important person', and had a reputation of being wise and kind. After meeting him the dreamer came away feeling that he had met a great and helpful man. Then he had the following dream:

> I see Mr X. His face looks quite different from what it did yesterday. I see a cruel mouth and a hard face. He is laughingly telling someone that he has just succeeded in cheating a poor widow out of her last few cents. I feel a sense of revulsion.

In referring to the dream, the dreamer said that he did have a feeling of disappointment when he had first walked in and seen Mr X's face. The impression disappeared as soon as Mr. X started his friendly conversation. Subsequent meetings bore out some of the facts of his dream, although not as extreme – but dreams are often exaggerated to draw attention. Checking out with others, he found they had also experienced impressions which they had not dared voice because Mr X's image had been so good.

Such dreams as this and my dream about the community rest on sensory information that has been suppressed. The dreams seem to come from nowhere, but in examining impressions it can be seen that the dreamer had the information but for one reason or another did not want to recognize it. The dream serves as a useful reminder, as well as illustrating the wider view of the unconscious.

The information picked up, but not consciously recognized, is shown in another dream described by Fromm. After meeting 'B' in real life, 'A' decides to take him on as a business partner. He has a dream in which he sees 'B' sitting in the common office. 'B' is going over the books and changing the figures in them to cover the fact that he has embezzled large sums of money. 'A' ignored the message in his dream, until it became no longer possible to do so, and much damage was done which could have been avoided.

Part of the difficulty in accepting our dreams is that not only are we taught to devalue them and identify with the waking personality, but that they may express things we would rather not be aware of. They remind us of buried feelings and parts of ourselves, so that we hardly recognize these feelings as ours and do not want to take responsibility for them, let alone act on them.

Here is another example of how a dream can illustrate very vividly a situation where a person is not willing to face what he unconsciously knows.[9] A man had been offered a job that would bring him a lot of money and prestige, but would involve him in violating principles that were important to him. In his conscious mind he argued that it would be better for his family if he were to take the higher paid job. To refuse would be egotistical and self-indulgent. Nevertheless he was not satisfied by his rationalizations and could not make up his mind until the night when he had a dream in which he was encouraged to drive up a steep road. The hill got more and more dangerous, but the dreamer could not stop because he could not turn round. Near the top his car stalled. The brakes would not work and the car rolled back over a precipice. He woke in terror. It was not difficult to work out the meaning of the dream because the person who had encouraged him to go up the steep path was a person who had sold out himself, was unhappy and had ceased to be creative.

There are numerous examples where dreams give us a jolt when we are unwilling to accept the evidence we have at our disposal. Even in the region of health, dreams pick up cues well before we have consciously allowed ourselves to recognize the signs of illness. A student of mine dreamt that he had a ring on his big toe that was giving him trouble. In reflexology the base of the big toe is believed to have a connection through the nervous system with the throat, so I asked him if he had any trouble with his throat. He said no, but three months later was diagnosed as having cancer of the throat. The signs were in the dream well before he had any conscious knowledge of his illness.

Sometimes acting on the dreams requires courage. A member of one of my dream groups dreamt that she was dying of cancer. The dream so startled her, that she decided to have a check on a lump which had been bothering her for a very long time. In fact it turned out to be not at all serious, but had she not been in the habit of paying attention to her dreams, she would have continued to push the information to the back of her mind instead of taking positive action.

In today's world logic, scientific proof, and so-called hard facts are generally considered more important than feelings. Yet there is increasing evidence that repressed feelings undermine our health and creativity. Heart disease has long been connected with stress and one of the other main killers of our time, cancer, is thought to be connected with certain personality types who have difficulty expressing their feelings. By culturally repressing the side of ourselves which emerges at night, we may be losing touch with the opportunity to be more in touch with our feelings and sources of inspiration and intuition, as well as our connectedness with the rest of humanity. In the examples of dreams given by Fromm and myself, the cost of ignoring the information can be seen. Carl Jung says that, 'Within each of us there is another whom we do not know. He speaks to us in dreams and tells us how differently he sees us from how we see ourselves. When we find ourselves in an insolubly difficult situation, this stranger in us can sometimes show us a light which is more suited to change our attitude fundamentally, namely just that attitude which has led us into the difficulty situation.'

In my work as a therapist, I try to encourage people to become less passive, and by gradually understanding and accepting innermost feelings, to have more conscious and aware choices. Calvin Hall,[10] who collected thousands of dreams, found that a very high percentage of dreams were unpleasant, many involving the dreamer in some kind of victim position. This passivity corresponds to some extent with the amount of choice we often feel we have in daily living, where important decisions are not in our hands.

There is a direct correlation between feelings of passivity in dreams and daily life. It is for this reason that I find working with dreams an important corrective, as, by working on the dream there is almost invariably a carry over into daily life. We do not need to have dreams of Einsteinian proportions to make a study of them worthwhile.

All the dream examples quoted above lent themselves quite easily to being understood, with the exception of the dream of the ring and the big toe, which needed some knowledge of physiology. In fact, I believe that most of us have an ability to understand dreams when given the opportunity. (I should add here that this applies to other people's more than our own. It always seems to be easier to fathom out what another person is up to rather than our own motives, especially when we are dealing with the more hidden parts of ourselves.) Imagining that we can only make use of our dream resources with expert help is another way of barring them from everyday life. Psycho-analysis has helped perpetuate that myth as well as helping to associate dreams with a need for treatment. In fact, as I shall show later in Chapter 7, children spontaneously intepret their own and each other's dreams. There may be times when a skilled dream interpreter is of value. But by and large I believe it is important not to let the expert replace our inner ability. I shall talk more about this as well as traditional ways of approaching the dream in the next chapter.

3.

WHAT DOES THIS DREAM MEAN?

'The patient does not need to have a truth inculcated into him. If we do that, we only reach his head; he needs far more to grow up to this truth, and in that way we reach his heart, and the appeal goes deeper and works more powerfully.'

C. Jung

'To experience a dream and its interpretation is very different from having a tepid rehash set before you on paper.'

C. Jung

'The dreamer *does* know what his dream means; only he does not know that he knows it and for that reason thinks he does not know it.'

S. Freud

'If it were not so paradoxical, one would almost call out to the dream interpreter: 'Do anything you like, only don't try to understand!'

C. Jung

'It is the dreamer himself who should tell us what his dream means . . .'

S. Freud

The Need to Look For Meaning

The struggle to come to terms with the dreaming part of ourselves is not new. Today we may do it by repressing or devaluing the dream, but historically people have always had their ways of lessening the effects of dreams. The

Talmud, for example, records a special cathartic ritual which could mitigate the power of an ominous dream.

The anxiety to protect oneself against bad dreams, which is found in most civilizations, has resulted in the classification of dreams into those with favourable and those with unfavourable images, as we saw in the first chapter. The latter were dealt with in a variety of ways, as for example 'cutting off' the unfavourable dreams by cutting off the hair with scissors! The Chinese would make offerings in the four directions, a classical gesture of politely expelling harmful things and beings. They also had the idea of Lie-Tseu, according to which, knowledge of causes destroys the fear, if not the effects, of the dream. This Freudian idea was inherent in the Taoist philosophy which held that mental troubles could be reduced by knowing their causes. In this way the power of the dream could be reduced and brought into the realm of waking life where things are 'understood'.

Lessening the power of a bad dream through sacrifice or ritual or understanding is, in different ways, an attempt to cope with the frightening and the unknown. It is for this reason, perhaps, that dream dictionaries have such popular appeal through the ages. By looking up symbols in a dictionary and finding meaning, the hope is to explain what seemed inexplicable. This need for meaning has, I think, its roots in a deep human need for order, purpose and intelligibility which the dream sometimes appears to threaten. One of the ways we can attempt to regain control is by interpretation.

Interpreting and Re-experiencing
The history of dream interpretation is very old, and both Jung and Freud talk of the interpretation of dreams. There is a danger, however, that the insights remain purely intellectual, and are not of lasting benefit to the dreamer because the feelings may have been bypassed. Jung was aware of this danger as the opening quotations of this chapter clearly show. Knowing why I do something does not necessarily help me. It can even increase my defences, as I add long elaborate explanations whilst I continue that

particular behaviour. For example I have known for some time on an insight/head level that I become angry with men who are in a superior position to me, but who will not admit their failings and hide behind their position. These feelings arise out of my relationship with my father, but this insight alone did not help me. It was not until I was ready to deal with my painful feelings of disappointment and betrayal that any change began to occur.

Many of the newer psychotherapies which broadly go under the heading of Humanistic Psychology do *not* interpret but allow the meaning to come from the dreamer. These therapies focus on re-experiencing the feelings and images of the dream as fully as possible. In this way, by working with the feelings, meaning will spontaneously arise and connections will be made that come from the dreamer himself. Working in this way avoids the pitfall of knowing what the dream means, making sense of the disturbing images, and leaving it there – like when you take a day trip to the Continent to sample the wares and then scuttle safely back home. Some of the techniques given in Chapter 5 will help to re-experience the dream more fully rather than interpret it. For the meantime, I would ask you to be aware of the almost unconscious urge to 'make sense' of the dream in an intellectual way only, an urge which leads us not only to put labels on our dreams but also on the dreaming process (for example seeing all dreams as 'meaningless' or 'rich sources of creativity'). Here are some recent examples to illustrate the differences between meaning and re-experiencing.

A woman in one of my dream groups had the following dream. 'I am in my bedroom and I become aware of an evil force coming in through the window. I know that if I don't keep it out, it will destroy me, but I am paralysed and wake up in fear.' I asked her how she understood the dream but she was not able to make any immediate connections. I then asked her if she could in any way connect the dream with the events of the day before. It transpired that she had had a row with her boyfriend and had gone to bed feeling bad, fearing that the relationship was becoming destructive. She connected the feelings that were with her when she went to bed with the dream and was very relieved. However, leaving it there added nothing to what she already knew – that the relationship was becoming destructive. The dream made her take notice, but the danger was that once she realized it was not a dream about evil, she would let its impact drop. Such questions as why she translated her feelings into an evil force, how she paralysed herself, what she was frightened would happen next if she hadn't woken herself up, remain unasked and unanswered. The 'meaning' obtained by connecting the feeling in the dream with unresolved feelings of the night before, could stop her asking such questions.

Here is another example. Some time ago, my partner Joan fell asleep after our lovemaking. In her dream our bed has caught fire from a cigarette which had been left there. She thinks X is in the bed with her. I asked her what she thought was the connection between her and X, and she had a flash of insight. Joan made a connection with X being unfaithful to her husband and her own feeling of being unfaithful to her ex-husband whilst we were making love. Joan had not realized how her old marriage was still affecting her and how much residual guilt she still had, even though she and her ex-husband had been separated and divorced for several years. I use this example to illustrate that even though Joan arrived at her own insight, transformed behaviour would not follow automatically. She would still need to work on her feelings towards her ex-husband. While the dangerous feelings expressed by the fire had been recognized, they had not been put out.

A final example concerns another woman in one of my dream groups. She dreamt that her daughter was four years old (in reality she is seventeen) and was struggling as hard as she could to prevent her mother from putting on her coat. Because the dreamer's daughter is not four years old, I made a guess that the dreamer might be struggling with her own internal four year old and the dreamer agreed, spontaneously adding that she had recently had an operation and wanted to be looked after, but was making it as difficult for people as her daughter was for her in the dream. Again a meaning had been arrived at, but the real work lay in taking it further and finding out more about that rebellious four year old and what she wanted.

Of course there are some dreams that need no interpretation as the experience of them is sufficent to produce transformation in the dreamer. The creative dreams mentioned in the second chapter would be such examples, where the dreamer wakes with an immediate insight that can be applied. Another such example is the dream of Dement in his book *Some Must Watch While Some Must Sleep*,[1] where he wakes up from a dream in which he sees himself dying of cancer from smoking too much. The dream is so real that he is relieved to wake up and find that it is not true, and the feeling is powerful enough to stop him from smoking any more.

In her book, *The Dream Game*,[2] Ann Faraday quotes Edgar Cayce, the American mystic who worked extensively with dreams, as saying that a dream is only properly understood when it leads to a change in behaviour. I take him to mean here that if the feelings in the dream have been fully experienced, inevitably there will be a carry over into everyday life, whereas if the insight is on an understanding level, all that will be gained is insight.

I was talking about this relationship between insight and change to a friend of mine who works with dreams and he told me of a woman he had met on holiday. She needed two sticks to hobble about as both her legs were paralysed. During the first four days of her holiday, the woman apparently miraculously regained the use of her legs and walked without the sticks. She had realized that she had been carrying a deep resentment for two years from the time when her son had got married. What had happened was that he had asked if he and his wife could stay with her for a couple of weeks while they looked for a place to live. They had since made no attempt to move out. Although the woman had felt resentful, she had never confronted her son with her feelings, as she had the ideal of Christian love. It was in this period that the paralysis of her legs had begun. The holiday had not only taken her away from home, but had also allowed her freedom from her suppressed feelings. She was certain that this freedom had allowed her legs to heal just as the buried resentment had caused the sickness. Her parting words were to the effect that she was going to ask her son to move out as soon as she got home. Although not connected with a dream, this would be an example of an insight 'properly understood', in Cayce's terms. Cayce also added that it was not as important to get the right solution as to learn the process by which the solution could be found.

To summarize the chapter so far, we can see how the anxiety evoked by dreams causes people to deal with them in different ways – by diminishing their importance, by suppressing them, by refusing to tell them and by trying to understand and make sense of them. Modern psychology aims to elicit more from the dreamer, especially in the area of feelings. Working like this leads on to meaning and change on a deeper level, which cannot arise from an intellectual understanding alone. The question of meaning takes on a different perspective in this way.

Our Understanding of Dreams

The recent move away from experts who interpreted dreams would not be able to gain ground if the ability to understand dreams intuitively was not more readily accessible than people had been led to believe. In dream groups where people are given permission to trust this part of themselves, deep intuitive understanding occurs. In this situation we tune into a universal language which, in Fromm's words, we have forgotten.

Some of the clearest evidence for this comes from experiments done under hypnosis. Subjects who had no knowledge of dream interpretation were given the hypnotic suggestion, 'you understand dreams'. They were then, in a hypnotic state, given dreams to interpret which they managed to do successfully. However when given the same dreams when not under hypnosis, the dreams did not make sense to them. I would guess that the ability to understand dreams is quite buried, and we do not allow ourselves access to it in normal circumstances. These experiments are described in *The New World of Dreams* by Woods and Greenhouse[3] and I will quote some of them.

It was suggested to one subject under hypnosis that as a child she had wet the bed and had been severely scolded by her mother. In response to this stimulus she dreamed of falling into a pond in winter and being severely scolded by her mother. The dream was then related to a second woman under hypnosis, who was entirely ignorant of the genesis of the dream. Without any hesitation the second subject said, 'Oh, that girl must have wet the bed', thus recovering the stimulus that had produced the dream. A second example, illustrating the sexual differentiation of symbols, is the following dream given for translation: 'A man is sitting in a dentist's chair while the dentist tries to pull his tooth. He pulls and pulls. The dreamer is in great pain when the dream ends'. Several subjects said the dream meant that a man was having a 'vital organ' cut off. When the dental patient was a woman, the dream was translated as 'giving birth to a baby'.

These experiments interested me as they confirmed my belief in the understanding of this common language. I did not believe, however, that this understanding could only be achieved under hypnosis, so I took the dreams to an evening class I was teaching. They were mostly comparative beginners who had come to an introductory class. Believing, however, as I do, that a good group can easily bring out people's inherent intuitive abilities, I read the dreams out and encouraged them to come up with suggestions of the meaning of the dreams, however absurd they might seem. In all cases they were able to guess at the original stimuli or situation which had evoked the dream.

I believe we all have an understanding of the symbolic language which appears not only in dreams, but also in myth, legend and fairy tale. I see my role as dreamworker as encouraging people to trust their intuition and understanding of this language. This understanding is, I think, not blocked by children. In Chapter 7 I look at children sharing dreams in a school setting and how remarkably easily they tune into each other. For the momemt here are some individual examples.

Our eleven-year-old had a dream one night and was reluctant to share it as we normally did. Finally he did. In the dream he was supposed to be taking part in a school race, but he had been left out of the heats although his younger brother had been included. I guessed he must have some idea of what the dream meant as he had been unwilling to share it, and asked him. He said that it was about his still being angry that the night before we had gone out without him after waiting for quite a time for him to turn up. On another occasion he had a dream in which there was a large swimming pool in the middle of his father's sitting room. He was splashing around in it, but his father told him off for making a mess. He said he knew that the dream was about being told off for eating noisily in the sitting room the day before. Finally, a friend told me of her son's dream in which he was suffocated by a fat woman falling on him. She was worried that he was telling her something about their relationship, but he assured her that it was to do with his feelings about school. Three weeks later he fainted there. My friend blamed herself for not listening to him more carefully as he had been quite sure of what the dream was referring to.

This understanding does not confine itself to children. An amusing example of how a person can understand a dream without ever reading anything about dreams concerns an uncle and aunt of mine. When my uncle heard that I was writing a book on dreams, he insisted on challenging me with the following dream. He is waiting for a lift, standing on the ground floor. A lady comes and joins him, and while they are in the lift together she asks him if there is any hot water. My uncle says he doesn't know. On getting out of the lift, my uncle goes into his flat and tries his taps and nothing comes out. (You might now like to hazard a guess about the possible meaning of the dream.) I am generally reluctant to interpret, leaving it as much as possible to the dreamer to come up with their own ideas. However, something in the manner in which he challenged me irked me and I asked him if he really wanted to know what the dream was about. He assured me he did, and so I told him it was a sexual anxiety dream. He laughed at me and said that the interpretation was ridiculous and that I had only to ask his wife to see this could not be true. I shrugged my shoulders and there we left it. Five minutes later he came back into the room to say that I was right. The day before he had been talking to a friend who had become impotent and this had aroused fears in my uncle as he too, like his friend, was getting past middle age.

Now the interesting part for me happened the next day – I was talking to my aunt and she mentioned that she had heard that I had interpreted her brother's dream. I told her the dream and I had barely finished when she burst out laughing and told me what she thought the dream meant. Without knowing anything other than that I had interpreted a dream of my uncle's, she came up with an almost identical interpretation. Of course she knows her brother and the way he feels, but she did also seem to have access to some idea of symbol interpretation.

As the above dream and the hypnosis experiments show, it would seem that there are some dreams that can be understood without reference to the dreamer and some where only the dreamer can shed light on the particular symbols.

Accidental and Universal Symbols

This paradox is explored in Fromm's section on symbols.[4] He talks about three kinds of symbols: the conventional, the accidental and the universal. A conventional symbol no longer has the connection between sound and object. The word 'table', for example, no longer has that connection even if there was once a connection between the sound and the object. Thus although millions of people would be able to connect the word with the object, someone who didn't speak English would not. A flag would also have that function – meaningful to particular people because of regular usage.

Accidental symbols, on the other hand, are totally personal, but there is also no intrinsic relationship between the symbol and the thing it symbolizes. For example, I connect the town of Malvern with the bitter-sweet experiences of my first girlfriend. Dreaming of Malvern could well remind me that I went to bed wishing that I was an adolescent again. There will not be many people who have this association. Accidental symbols are very important in understanding dreams as they comprise much of the personal associations of the dreamer and without these associations it would be difficult, if not impossible, to understand the dream.

By contrast, there is a direct connection between the universal symbol and what it represents. A conventional symbol might make sense to people of one culture, but a universal symbol has a wider significance in that it is related to our bodily sensations. Thus the experience of falling is fearful no matter where we come from, as is the fear of being chased or attacked. Within these experiences there will be variations. Thus the sun has universal properties of heat, light, etc. but its importance in a particular culture will vary according to whether you are living in a desert or a cold climate. As well as differing emphases on universal symbols according to geography, the context of the symbol is very important. Water is necessary for life and has certain properties, but its meaning in a dream will obviously vary according to whether it is a tidal wave destroying, or a gentle river carrying you along. In the examples quoted of hypnotic suggestions about dreaming about wetting the bed, we are dealing with a bodily function, which made dream inter-pretation easier – such as the example of my uncle's dream in which there was no water coming out of the taps. This dream might have had a totally different meaning if there had been a water strike – although the fact that he was talking about it to a woman in a lift would still direct me to the original interpretation no matter what the outside context.

I would like to end this section with an example of how a social situation (accidental symbol level) can be translated into body language (universal symbol level). A young girl was given as a stimulus a situation in which, falsely accused by a friend of cheating in an examination, she became very angry but because of circumstances was unable to deny the accusation. The subject then dreamed that a dentist was trying to pull her tooth despite her frightened protests that the nurse had taken the anaesthetic out of the wrong bottle. In her dream the humiliating accusation is portrayed as bodily assault. We see how a familiar dream symbol (tooth pulling) can portray a variety of human experiences, and how there is at one and the same time often a personal trigger which can be translated into a more universal language readily understood by others.

Different Levels in the Dream

This brings me to the point that the same dream may be operating on different levels. In the section on re-experiencing versus interpreting I suggested that often interpretation deals with one level only, and bypasses the level of deeper feeling. I would like to look at this idea more closely.

A few years ago my Jungian analyst told me the following example of a patient's dream. A girl dreamt that she was back at school and had been put down into a lower class because there was a piece of work appropriate to an earlier age group which she had failed to do. This made her so angry that she ran away from school planning revenge. She found herself lost in a desert and woke up in terror. She told my analyst she knew what the dream meant. At her secretarial work she had been taken off a responsible job because her boss said she was treating the work too superficially. The analyst asked about the desert and the girl replied that at first she thought of leaving when her boss had said what he did, but then she had become scared that she wouldn't find another job and that would be like a desert. It would have been easy to have left the dream there as the dreamer felt satisfied with this 'first level' interpretation. However the analyst thought there might be more to it than that and asked the girl how she had been told of the down-grading in her dream. The girl became uneasy and embarrassed and said that the headmistress had invited her to tea and explained very patiently why it was necessary and that it would be an advantage to her in the end. The analyst then interpreted that maybe the headmistress was part of her who was telling her that she needed to go back into her childhood years and get a piece of work done without running away from therapy. The girl nodded and said that she had come with the intention of stopping therapy because she hated going into 'all that dream stuff'. Acknowledging the inner wisdom of her own headmistress, she was able to begin to explore the desert of her own psyche which she had been afraid to do before.

In this example, the analyst was able to use her skill to go behind the first level of the dream. As well as different levels, there do seem to be different kinds of dreams. As Jung said, 'Dreams may contain ineluctable truths, philosophical pronouncements, illusions, wild fantasies, memories, plans, anticipations, irrational experiences, even telepathic visions, and heaven knows what besides'.

Different Kinds of Dream: Why Classify?

The idea of classifying dreams is not new. Virgil, the Roman poet, talked about dreams coming through the gates of horn and ivory – the first being true dreams and the latter being deceiving and illusory. The ancients were particularly keen to find out the origin of a dream – whether it was from God or the Devil.

What advantages does classifying have for us now? On the one hand it cuts across rigid theoretical boundaries. On the other hand classifications are functions of the waking mind, not the dreaming one. The danger is always the Procrustean one of trying to make dreams and images fit into a particular waking category. It is best, in the words of Strephon Williams, to 'Set aside your categories, even your useful ones, and look at the dream as a fresh, original experience. The meaning of a dream does not depend on the category you give it, but what you do to re-experience it'.[5] So perhaps what is needed are techniques to enable us to re-experience the dream, rather than categories and dictionaries which give meanings.

Although it is true that classifying dreams is a function of the waking mind, there are nevertheless some advantages in it. For example, many people dream of having cancer. If the dreamer is unaware of the symbolic nature of dreams, but has a literal view, this dream will cause considerable anxiety. For example, a man dreamed he had cancer of the throat and was coughing up maggots. When he worked on the dream and re-experienced the feelings, he was able to get in touch with the fear that remained with him from a childhood tonsil operation. Releasing the fear cured a long-standing neck tension. The dream symbolized the negative feelings as maggots and cancer. If he had considered the dream as a health dream, he would have caused himself unnecessary anxiety. On the other hand, as we have seen (in the example of the big toe dream), some people are warned of physical illness prior to its expression as a symptom.

The question then arises as to how you can tell the difference, not only with health dreams, but those concerning death and ones where some misfortune is about to happen. There are no absolute rules except to say that usually dreams about death are symbolic. What must always be taken into account is the context in which the dream is dreamt. By this I mean the remnants of the day, somatic stimuli, the physical environment, the relationships of the dreamer, and the dreamer's time of life. Thus in the example of the evil force coming through the window (page 31) we see many of these factors operating.

However, and this may come with practice and confidence, my main source of knowledge is the 'feeling' I get from someone's dream. I hold all the different possibilities as hypotheses. In training people to listen to dreams, I encourage them to be aware of how they are listening. How the dream is worked with will depend at least as much on the listener or therapist as the actual dream. It is therefore very important that the therapist be very aware of his own ideas and preconceptions in order to enable him to be as receptive as possible. There is nothing worse than having a dream butchered to fit into someone else's theory or be dealt with in other insensitive ways. I mention the importance of listening as carefully as possible because I believe the dreamer very often knows the meaning of his own dream and will give you hints in the telling. Here is an example of a dream told to me in great distress, which will indicate some of the ways I listen to someone's dream.

In this dream, a lady told me that she had gone into a building with her two year old son and somewhere inside she had lost him. The next thing she knew was that he had fallen from the seventh floor and died. Now this dream could be taken on several levels and as she had stopped me in panic in the coffee break, I only had a few minutes. First I checked up on the external level. I asked her on which floor she lived in real life. She lived on the fourth. I did not think the building had anything to do with the outer world as it was dark, disused and unfamiliar. I asked about her relationship with her son and when she said it was good, I believed her. I then said that I had no way of knowing for sure, but I did not think the dream was really about her son, but about part of herself. I asked her to think about what had happened seven years ago, or when she was seven. She went away greatly relieved. I had not promised that the dream was not about her son, but had treated his death as being symbolic and had asked her about her own life. In any case, apart from watching over her son carefully, there was nothing on an external level she could do, so I was playing reasonably safe in trying to guide her internally, and certainly she felt relieved. The following week she came back and told me she had been married for seven years and the marriage was going badly wrong. Her child was obviously aware of this, and unless she did something he was going to be affected.

Looking at this dream in more detail, it would seem that I was able to tune into the right level in a way that was useful to the dreamer, as she went and had some marriage guidance counselling. With dreams of death, illness and disaster it is important to be able to distinguish whether they are anxiety dreams, warning dreams or precognitive dreams (dreams about something that will happen). The latter dream was a warning dream, not a precognitive dream as the dreamer feared. How I tell the difference depends on how I feel when someone tells me the dream. With a precognitive dream, I get a real chill running down my spine – probably picking up the dreamer's own intuitions.

A similar distinction needs to be made between positive dreams and wish fulfillments. For example, a woman with cancer dreamt that she would improve two weeks after a specific form of treatment about which she had been hesitating. In fact this did happen, but the dream could very easily have been a wish fulfilment dream. Again I can only offer the same guidelines as for warning/ precognitive/anxiety dreams.

Gathering together some of the above information, I would classify dreams as follows: nightmares, shadow dreams, recurring dreams, creative dreams, problem-solving dreams, precognitive dreams, warning dreams, lucid dreams, wish-fulfilment dreams, clearing dreams, 'big dreams', information dreams, communication dreams and social dreams. By making this categorization, I am deliberately cutting across Freudian, Jungian and other schools. I am also saying by my choice of category how I listen to dreams and some of my ideas and theories of dreams.

Nightmares. Calvin Hall[6] found that dreams were more unpleasant than not. The nightmare, as opposed to the anxiety dream, I classify as the one where you wake up in fear or terror, often from being chased, suffocated or falling. Often these nightmares can be remembered in great detail years later. These dreams are potentially very useful dreams, although they do not seem so at the time. Generally what has happened is that something has been ignored in everyday life and the dream is a reminder that this situation has become intolerable. It is as if the energy has turned back in on itself because it has been denied expression. For example if anger is not expressed or channelled creatively, the feelings will lie buried and emerge in a dream, sometimes as anger or rage but sometimes in the form of anger directed towards oneself. There are techniques which help us use the energies in a nightmare creatively. These are described in Patricia Garfield's *Creative Dreaming*[7]. Our society values the rational and does not provide us with ways of dealing with these often terrifying forces other than sleeping pills and some comment on best forgetting about it all.

Similar to these are what can be called *shadow dreams*. These reveal parts of ourselves that we keep locked away in everyday life so that they come back to haunt us at night. The murderer, Nazi, thief, exhibitionist, and coward are some examples. These *may* be nightmares in that the shadow could be turned against us, but what can be disturbing is the pleasure we take in doing things we would not normally do. It is sometimes very difficult for people to accept the shadow part as part of themselves –

for example a woman who had escaped from the Germans was outraged when I suggested she speak as one of the Nazis in her dream. She later came to accept that she had a strong persecutory part in her dream. For so long she had only allowed herself to be seen as a victim and the work on her shadow side was an important step in the reintegration of part of her personality.

A third kind of usually unpleasant dream connected with the nightmare is the *recurring dream*. These can vary from occuring every night, so that the dreamer is frightened to go to sleep, to happening once every few years. As I understand it, this dream also comes to remind us that something in our lives has still not been dealt with. In fact the dream is an attempt to find resolution. Thus the man who dreamt of having cancer and maggots in his throat had for many years also dreamt of having his throat attacked in a variety of ways. When he finally traced the origin to his tonsil operation, the recurring dream stopped.

Creative/problem-solving dreams. I have bracketed these together because in both types of dream the dreaming mind has shown possibilities that the waking mind has not thought of. The sorts of dreams mentioned at the beginning of Chapter 2 are not for the most part the average dream. In fact they have been peddled in dream literature because they are so unusual. However problem-solving dreams do occur quite often. For example, I had been worried for some time about proposed cuts in my part-time job as a lecturer in counselling. All my conscious efforts were devoted to fighting them. I had a dream in which I was teaching some students I didn't know in a building which I did not recognize. I woke up thinking that it was time I started my own course, which I am now in the process of doing.

Precognitive dreams. These are dreams that tell of something which later actually occurs. Often these have a very simple explanation, such as the example given in Chapter 2 (page 24) where the dreamer obviously was picking up clues which he wasn't allowing himself to know consciously. However there are some dreams where such explanations are not so easy to come by. Dreams of disasters such as Aberfan by those who had never even heard of the place are documented. There are plenty of opportunities to dismiss these as coincidence, wishful thinking (e.g. fitting the dream into the events after they have happened) but these all deny the possibility that the dreaming mind is able to process information in a way that is different to that of the conscious mind. Why the dreaming mind usually operates in a way that often predicts bad events rather than good is that perhaps in times of stress we are thrown back on a more primitive part of ourselves.

Warning dreams. These may come in the form of nightmares or precognitive dreams. Health dreams would fit into this category. As with all dreams, much depends on what is done with them. The advice can be taken or ignored. A few years ago I was thinking of starting a relationship. In a dream I saw the person talking behind my back. I decided to hold back and later saw that my anxieties about this person, which I had not allowed myself to know consciously, were well-founded.

Lucid dreams. These are dreams where you know you are dreaming in the actual dream. Usually you are in the middle of a dream and a thought will flash through, 'Hey this is a dream'. People then react in different ways, trying out all sorts of possibilities like flying or having a sexual experience, or experimenting to see how the dream state differs from the waking state by throwing a glass against a wall to see if it breaks. This kind of dream has received much publicity recently. Personally, I think the desire to be lucid in a dream is an attempt to control the dream state before being receptive to the actual messages that can be learnt. James Hillman[8] contrasts going into the underworld to plunder, like Hercules, as opposed to learn. However there are cases where dream control by becoming lucid has helped deal with recurring nightmares, so there may be uses for trying to achieve lucidity in a dream.

Wish-fulfilment dreams. These are often children's dreams. 'I dreamt that you said I could have as many sweets as I liked' (after a day in which the child was rebuked for spending money on sweets) or 'I dreamt that I was riding a new bicycle'. Freud maintained that all dreams were wish fulfilments, only we become more adept at disguising them as we grow older. I do not believe this. However, it can be important to recognize a wish-fulfilment dream. For example, a woman who has feelings of inferiority in everyday life has dreams in which she is very successful. She chooses to take the dreams at face value, and believing her feelings of inferiority have been dealt with stops therapy, only to find that her success in dreams was illusory.

Clearing dreams. I give this name to what are probably a large proportion of dreams. A well-known researcher described how some of the night life is attempting to erase the day's events, like a computer erasing its programs in order to be reprogrammed. He says that there is so little time for clearing in everyday life which is lived at such a fast pace, and because our senses are so bombarded, that most of the clearing has to take place at night, with the result that other dream functions, like for example having 'big' or 'transformative' dreams are not so readily available.

'Big' dreams. These are the ones that stay with you for years and can often be remembered in exact detail years later. The intensity of these dreams gives them a religious or spiritual dimension. In non-industrialized societies, people will fast for days to try to get such dreams.

Information dreams. This class could cover all dreams. However, I mean it in the sense that the dream does not need interpretation, but gives information about part of yourself, others or the world that is easy to see directly, and which you may not have allowed yourself consciously to know. Thus if I dream that the brakes on my car have failed, this could be telling me to check my brakes; if I dream about X, it could be giving information about X. This means taking the person or object not as a symbol but for itself.

Dreams for Communication. This sort of dream often

happens when you know that you are likely to be sharing the dream with someone, say a therapist, or other members of a group. In this kind of dream, it is not only the dream that has to be watched for, but the message the dream conveys to the listener. To take a crude example: if I have a sexual dream about X, in telling her about it I am not only working with the dream, but indirectly saying something about me and her through the dream telling, something which I may not have been able to say otherwise. When members of a group tell me 'psychic dreams', whilst not invalidating the truth of their experience, I sometimes see this as a communication to the group that the dreamer believes he/she is 'special'.

Social Dreams. These are dreams about the social order in which we live. Carl Jung dreamt of rivers of blood before the First World War. He thought this related to his own personal pathology until the war broke out and he realized he had forseen it. The Bible distinguishes between dreams and visions – the former are personal but the latter have to be communicated and roughly correspond to my category of social dreams. In less industrialized societies this kind of dream is given great significance, where dreams can relate to the good of the whole tribe. The absence of an institutionalized sharing has meant that by and large the dream does not feed back into society, but becomes another facet of individuality. It has also meant that most people have lost touch with dream language with the result that, like so many other functions, it has become the terrain of specialists.

In looking at these classifications, which are personal and in no way exhaustive or comprehensive, I want to show some of the different facets of dreaming. When listening to a dream, I am aware that the dream could be in any of the above categories, and the way I choose to work with it will depend on the kind of dream it might be. The danger of interpretation is that even if correct, it only gives one of many possibilities, and thus brings the dreamwork to what Jeremy Taylor[9] has called premature closure, i.e. being content with having found *the* meaning as opposed to a meaning. We see these levels operating in the following dream told to me by a cousin. She dreams that a friend of hers who is about to be married is wearing a wedding dress which is absolutely beautiful at the front, but there is nothing at the back and her friend does not realise this. My cousin is shocked. The dream could be: a) my cousin's perception of her friend – that she is all front; b) some deep intuition about the marriage which may be true and is not just her projection; c) her feelings about her own marriage or self as she is also about to get married soon; d) in telling this dream to her friend, she might be communicating some message to her friend via the dream and the telling. It could be a warning or an expression of competition. In fact, aspects of each one struck some kind of chord for my cousin, but it would have been easy to have just stuck to one.

Dream dictionaries. In an attempt to understand the meaning of dreams, people have had recourse to dream dictionaries of various sorts. I have no doubt that some of the better ones do have something of use to say about universal symbols, given the distinction I stated earlier about universal and accidental symbols. However so much is lost in doing this, that these dictionaries probably do more harm than good. We lose the place the symbol has in the dream as a whole, the feeling a dreamer has about it. Dream dictionaries can instil a false sense of security in the interpreter and stop any fuller understanding. For example, by reducing all objects that are pointed to phallic symbols, they help force the dream into one particular mould. There is also the added danger that they reduce the authority of the dreamer over his own dream, by looking outside to an arbitrary source. Opening one dictionary at random I see under the heading of Steps, 'Usually the different steps taken in any undertaking. The first step towards marriage is courtship, the next engagement and so on'. In fact this says very little. Do the steps lead up or down? Are they steep and do they, as in some dreams, get narrower? How did the person in the dream feel about the steps? Often they are associated with fear – leading to nowhere or down to a basement, for example.

Dream Themes. A common approach to understanding dreams is not only to look at symbols, but to look at themes such as missing a train, looking for a room, falling, flying, running from a pursuer, losing teeth, brakes failing, appearing naked in public, etc. Such an approach offers more scope than simple symbol substitution in that the themes involve more action than a symbol on its own. It is therefore possible to make pretty accurate guesses about a dream – say recognizing that brakes failing means loss of control – but the usual dangers of fitting an interpretation into a dream still apply. For example, in one popular book, under 'missing a train', the interpretation is given of the journey through life to the grave and the dream is supposed to reflect the dreamer's unconscious wish to reassure himself against the fear of death. By missing the train he says to himself 'I shall not die'. Now it is true to say that most people are afraid of death, so this interpretation could be made quite safely for a variety of reasons. The question of where missing the train fitted into the dream, how the person felt on waking, whether it is a recurring dream, where the dreamer was trying to get to are all ignored. Taking another example, appearing naked in a dream would have very different meanings for a Jesuit priest and a model.

Dream series. By recording and working with a series of dreams, it becomes possible to watch for patterns and developments in your dreams over a length of time. This allows for the deepening of any meanings that may have emerged, correcting any ideas and watching to see if the relationships in your dreams remain constant or change. I noticed that there was an undercurrent of anxiety in most of my dreams no matter what the symbols or themes. I had not seen this so clearly by taking the dreams in isolation.

Day Residue. A useful question to ask in working with dreams is, 'Why did I (you) have this dream now?' Several times people will try and 'explain' the dream by saying 'Oh, I dreamt about X because I saw him on television'. This does not explain why out of the mass of everyday stimuli, the dreamer chose X. There is always more to it than this superficial 'reason'.

To sum up the chapter so far, I have tried to show that a) we all have an intuitive understanding of the language of dreams; b) dreams can be of different types which cut across the boundaries of Freudian, Jungian thought etc; c) the same dream can operate on many levels and d) interpreting dreams can often be a way of bringing dreamwork to premature closure, often arising from the need to control by understanding.

An additional danger in looking for meaning is that it can take the authority away from the dreamer and leave too much in the hands of an outside authority – be it book or expert. The sort of skills that are needed are the ability both to follow the dream images and to get a feel for the dream as a whole. I do not think there is any harm in knowing some of the stock interpretations as long as they are held as tentative hypotheses and not allowed to obscure the active listening to the dream. This active listening (which I first described on page 41) will be enlarged on in the second half of the book.

The social side of symbols and interpretation. In the different kinds of dreams, my last two categories were communication dreams and social dreams. These aspects of dreaming have been comparatively neglected in dream literature. I would like to end the chapter with a story of how the power of dream interpretation can be misused and the danger of giving away authority. The story is called the 'Dream of the Cracked Granary'.[10] It concerns a woman who came to Rabi Eleizer and said to him, 'I saw in a dream that the granary of my house came open in a crack'. He answered, 'You will conceive a son'. She went away and that is what happened. She dreamed the same dream again and told it to Rabbi Eleizer who gave the same interpretation and that is what happened. She dreamed the same dream a third time and looked for Rabbi Eleizer. Not finding him, she told the dream to his disciples. They answered her, 'You will bury your husband'. And that is what happened. Rabbi Eleizer, surprised by the lamentations, enquired what had gone wrong. His disciples told him what had happened. He cried out, 'Wretched fools! You have killed that man. Is it not written, "As he interpreted to us, so it was"?' (Genesis 41 : 13)

What, it may be asked, is the point behind this rather unlikely Talmudic story? In post-biblical literature the idea was put forward that the dream was unimportant and that it was the interpretation that counted, becoming itself the effective forecast and thereby forcing reality to follow suit. This view undoubtedly suited the rabbis who used it to mould religious, social and political thought and behaviour, and teachers were able to appeal to the popular imagination through dream interpretations. What the story illustrates for me is that although dreaming is private, dream interpretation is a social act and there is a complex relationship between dream, dreamer, the telling of the dream, listener and outcome. This point is very relevant for therapy when there are dangers of interpreting through our familar frameworks. Patients are often very adept at picking up what our biases are, and it is well known that patients in Freudian analysis have Freudian dreams, and those in Jungian analysis Jungian dreams. All these factors have to be taken into account when working with dreams. In other words, dream interpretation also has a social context which can define the meaning. In laboratory experiments on sleep, subjects have been found to tell different parts of dreams to people according to their relationship with the listener.

I have begun to move towards the social side of dreaming because I believe that for too long the dream has been treated as an entity in itself. However for myself and others, interest first started in working with one's own dreams and the next two chapters will explore how to remember, record and work on your own dream.

4.

REMEMBERING
AND RECORDING

'Look out! Watch! Listen! A dream is dreaming through you'
Laurens van der Post in Parabola[1]

In Chapter 2 I examined some of the most likely reasons
for forgetting dreams. These included how quickly a
dream can fade from consciousness, the difficulty of
translating the largely pictorial images of dreams into
spoken and written language, the different personality
types, the tendency to repress unpleasant or disturbing
material, and the lack of cultural reinforcement to either
remember or share. I believe there is another reason at
least as important as any of the above.

Motivation
Given that we dream on average five times a night, it is no
longer possible to maintain 'I don't dream'; the evidence
since 1953 and the discovery of REM sleep is overwhelming.
What I have noticed, however, is that one of the factors
that differentiates recallers from non-recallers is motivation.
For some recall is easy, but for those who do not remember
my first question is, 'How much do you want to?' You may
remember that I quoted people who have remembered
their dreams well and come to a group and no longer
remember them. Later when their recall comes back they
acknowledge that they had forgotten because they were
not sure they wanted to share their dreams with the group.

My own view is that if you do not remember your dreams over a period of time, you do not want to. At first, this seems a little dogmatic. Often I hear people say they really want to, but have no time etc. but I still feel confident of my ground. Not remembering sometimes has a protective function. For example whilst writing this book my dream recall has dropped dramatically. Ann Faraday in *The Dream Game* reported a similar occurrence. For my part, I already have too much material with which to cope. I do not want any more. In the groups mentioned above, I think it is quite appropriate that people 'test out the water' first, and not recalling dreams is one way. So I do not make negative judgments about non-recall although I do say that motivation is crucial.

If you would like to accept my challenge, you might like to try this exercise. It involves finishing the sentence 'I don't want to remember my dreams because . . .' Here are some examples from people with whom I have tried the exercise. 'I don't want to remember my dreams because I am frightened of what I may find out.' 'I don't want to remember my dreams because there are more important things in my life right now.' Try listing as many endings as possible and then going through them to see how many stand up to close questioning. In my example of not remembering while I am doing the book, my partner confronted me and I realized it was part of my excuse of 'life will begin again after the book is finished' and my recall has returned.

Having offered the challenge of motivation, there are still some very useful tips for recallers and non-recallers alike. If, like me, you recoil from anything that smacks of regular discipline you have my sympathies. However, I recommend buying a book in which to record your dreams. This book will need to be kept by your bedside ready for a dream to be recorded, along with a bedside lamp or small torch so that you don't have to get up and put on the light in the middle of the night. Tapes are another possible means of recording dreams, but I have found that I never made the effort to transcribe them later, so that what proved to be easier initially actually gave less results.

Before Sleep

However you choose to record, having set up the equipment, the next step is to pay attention to how you go to sleep. I choose this time to write up my day's events which acts as an impetus for writing the dreams later. This time is also very good for positive suggestion, e.g. saying to yourself as you drift off, 'Tonight I will remember my dreams', or 'I will wake up after I have had a dream and record it'. You can also visualize yourself waking up and recording a dream. Paying attention to how you go to sleep is important because your last thoughts before going to sleep will have quite an influence on your dreams, as will your mood. Here is an example of how both can influence the content of the night. It also shows that it is not always necessary to have a dream to work on.

Teri, one of the students I teach on Mondays, attended the dream group regularly. On the Saturday night she had had six dreams which she had written down. As she knew that I liked to work with dreams from the previous night, she had gone to bed on the Sunday eager for dreams to bring to the group on Monday. She awoke on Monday morning not remembering and was very disappointed. She shared this experience with the group and with her consent I decided to try an experiment. I asked her to lie down, close her eyes and imagine going to sleep. I asked her to go through her whole bedtime ritual – picturing her bedroom, brushing her teeth, undressing, getting into bed and so on. I then asked her to be in touch with any feelings and thoughts as she was doing this and to come up with an image. She came up with the image of a circus which I asked her to follow in her mind's eye. In this circus she was a clown who had to pass under a ladder. Every time she did this a child in the school where she taught poured a bucket of water over her. Suddenly she realized why she had not remembered. On Sunday night she had been excited about having dreams to share, but she now remembered feeling very anxious about going into school the next day and the anxiety had blotted out her dreams. The positive results from sharing this dream/fantasy will be described in Chapter 7, but for the moment the important issue is that thoughts and feelings before going to sleep will affect dreams and dream recall.

In the Night
Once you have prepared yourself for sleep, complete with diary or tape recorder by your bedside, and have given yourself a suggestion, the next step in the process could well be waking up in the middle of the night with a dream. If you do, my suggestion is that you go over it once or twice and then record it. Even if you review the dream over and over again and think that you could not possibly forget it in the morning, the chances are that you will. Research shows that only five minutes after a dream finishes, recall of it breaks up into fragments and ten minutes after a dream, recall is almost if not completely gone. I and others have learnt from experience that no matter how sure you are that you will not forget, recall of the dream will have gone by the morning.

In the Morning
If you do not wake up in the middle of the night, or record a dream from then, the most likely time is first thing in the morning. In fact this is the dream you are most likely to remember, partly because it is the longest (see page 20) and partly because it is the closest to waking consciousness in terms of depth of sleep. Again go over the dream in your mind's eye before beginning to write it down. Try not to move as research shows that movement can impair recall. Make sure that you have enough time to record it and are not dashing off to work, as again it will quickly fade as the day's events take over.

If you do not have a dream from this time in the morning, lie still and notice the mood you wake up in and any thoughts you may have. Remember your last thoughts before going to sleep and see if these trigger off any associations. If nothing comes, try simply doodling on your pad or in your diary. This will capture your mood and again may spark off memories. Incidentally, whether you record dreams regularly or not, paying attention to your mood on awakening is very important as this mood often stays with you for the rest of the day. If you can recapture the source of it as the student I described did, then there is less chance of being adversely affected for the rest of the day if you wake up feeling bad.

At one time I was making a mandala of my dreams by colouring in a pattern taken from *The Dreamwork Manual* by Strephon Kaplan Williams.[2] I noticed how differently I coloured in each night's sleep. So I suggested to a member of a group who could not remember his dreams that he think of a colour on awakening. He thought this a very strange idea, but as he couldn't remember a dream he thought of the colour yellow. This made him think of the sun, and as we worked on this association in the group he remembered a fragment of a dream he had had the previous night where the sun was hidden behind a cloud. We explored this a little more and he got in touch with his fears of darkness and his own darkness. Acting on intuition I took up the pun son/sun and he was able to work on his relationship with his father (he was the son left under a cloud) and his relationship with me as group leader (father). He made a connection between the two of us and the authority issues he had with us both.

This leads me to another important point. Do not dismiss any fragment of a dream as being unimportant. Like the example above a single fragment can lead to working in quite some depth. In fact when I work with people's dreams I usually find these little snippets the most fruitful. They often capture the essence of a person's current situation. Moreover it is the waking mind that judges whether a fragment is important, or relevant. Many times I have heard people introduce their dreams with a value judgement – nonsense, boring, meaningless. Sometimes this is a desire to protect themselves from criticism or because they are unfavourably comparing their dreams with other people's or even their own previous dreams which seem more exciting. My own view is that there is nothing that cannot be worked with providing you have the right tools. So be aware of wanting to edit out parts of dreams when recording.

If You Still Don't Remember

A final idea for those who have difficulty remembering their dreams is to try and dialogue with them. This can either be in written form or by using two cushions. This technique is one of the standard techniques of Gestalt therapy. It may at first sight seem strange to put your dreams onto an empty cushion and address them, but this Gestalt technique is the most powerful for working with dreams, remembered or not. Start with a question, for example, 'Dreams, why have you not come to me recently?' or 'I would like to get to know more about you – how can I do that?' Then go over to the cushion, become the dreams and reply. The dreams might reply with something like 'Whenever I do come to you, you don't take any notice. You wake up in the morning rushing and planning the day ahead. You won't even give me five minutes of your time' or, 'We are always available, but we think you are a little frightened of discovering something about yourself, so you would rather not know about us'. Move back to your original cushion, reply and gradually let a dialogue ensue. The two cushions often have two very distinct voices, a different body position and a different mood or energy. Sometimes a parent/child dialogue develops with the dream voice telling the other off for not listening to it. However this is only one of a number of combinations and I suggest you notice which voices the two cushions develop. The same thing can be done in written form. For example, in the reply to the dreams words 'You won't give me five minutes of your time', your reply might be, 'You're right. I have been preoccupied with other things. I'll try harder and make more space in the morning and follow out the procedures in this book'. Here you are nearer to a parent/child relationship of 'I'll try harder'. It is unlikely that this is a true resolution – the child part is trying to placate and may with an effort of will manage one half-hearted attempt before giving up again. Make sure you reach a conclusion that feels right, is without guilt and that is realistic. For example, do not feel you have to record all your dreams every day. I certainly don't!

Keeping a Record

A systematic way of writing up your dreams helps recall. As I mentioned earlier some people like tapes. Not only is it easier to record initially, but in writing them up insights suddenly pop up – just as they often do in simply telling someone. However for most people some sort of diary is the best way to record. Obviously you can make it in any form you like, but here are some suggestions.

First have a page for the day's events. These need only take up a few lines. Not only will they have some bearing on the night's dreams, but regularly writing up the day's events will act as a spur for remembering dreams. On the opposite page write the date and then record the dreams, leaving a space between each one if you remember more than one at a time (it does happen). Then I suggest you write your mood when awakening and the different moods you felt in the dream. I also recommend giving the dream a title as this will help fix the dream in your memory for later use, and possibly highlight some important aspect. At this stage you can record any thoughts or draw anything that suggests itself to you. Go over the dream once it is written, visualizing it if you can, and see if you have omitted anything. Then if you have time, go on to some of the techniques described in the next chapter.

Sharing

I started the chapter with a section on motivation and I would like to say that the biggest incentive I have for recording my dreams is having someone to share them with. I do not as a rule have any difficulty in remembering them (except when writing books!) and have diaries collected over the years. However I never manage to keep them for more than three months at a time, unless I have a regular place to share dreams. Working on my own is valuable to show patterns and themes, and I have learnt much. But for me nothing replaces regular dream sharing. This seems to be true for other people as well and the process deepens the more the same people share and work on their own and others' dreams over a period of time. However, I do not want to underestimate the value of beginning on one's own, and will describe some of the techniques I have found most useful.

5.

WAYS OF WORKING ON YOUR OWN

The main focus of this book is on sharing dreams as I think that most can be gained from dreamwork by sharing it with receptive people who can act as some kind of mirror. However for a variety of reasons this may not be possible, so in this chapter I will be suggesting methods of re-experiencing and understanding dreams by yourself. Although I have borrowed many of the methods from other dreamwriters, I have tried them all myself and will indicate how I have found them useful.

Of course, some dreams do not need working on. Their messages are clear and non-symbolic and do not have to be decoded, or the feelings are so powerful that changes in behaviour follow simply by having the dream. For example, at a very simple level, I woke up one morning at four-thirty knowing that I had left my library ticket in one of the books I had returned. I was not even aware that I had lost it. Why my dreaming mind should have bothered to give me this information I do not know, but it was accurate.

To give a slightly more complex example, a friend of mine was going to buy a house and saw two that, consciously, she liked equally. She dreams of one house looking dark and cramped, the other she sees with plants in the windows, and generally bright and well looked after. She checks out, and realizes she has indeed been suppressing some of her doubts about the first house as it was more conveniently located. I have often realized what my feelings about people are through dreams. These dreams do not need interpreting, just listening to as some of those described in Chapter 2 which I have classified as information dreams. For the most part, however, dreams have to be decoded as we are not used to their language.

Thematic Approach

In the last chapter I suggested giving each dream a title as it helps to fix the dream in your memory and can sum up the essence of a dream. A similar idea is to look for the theme in a dream. The thematic approach, as it is known, does not attempt to look for the meaning in the symbols. Rather it looks at the relationships between parts of the dream. Here is a simple example from a recent dream. In the dream I am admiring a beautifully ornate carved set of sewing drawers that belong to a friend of mine. I am surprised that he owns them. Without the theme approach I might focus on the symbols of the drawers. The theme approach focuses mainly on the verbs and turns the nouns into generalizations. It attempts to find the theme in a few words. Thus, my dream becomes Someone is admiring Something. By not focusing on the drawers, I realize that the essence of the dream is my admiration, and behind that some hidden envy of my friend which I had not previously recognized. (I am also aware that it is possible to see the drawers and my friend as representing some part of myself, but for the moment this level looks useful.) By turning pronouns into someone and objects into something, the relationships between the parts are highlighted. These could get obscured if symbols are looked at in detail. This thematic approach is then taken further, to relate the theme to everyday life. In my particular case, I do not have much trouble in recognizing the theme of envy, although I had not consciously related it to this particular person. More can be done with the dream (e.g. going further into the symbol of the drawers) but this approach is very useful for quickly going to the heart of the dream. It also gives you an opportunity to see how dreams with widely differing symbols can have the same themes. I have found this extremely useful.

'Following the Dream Ego'

A very similar technique is to ask the question, 'What am I doing in my dream?' 'Am I running, playing, struggling, eating, etc?' Strephon Williams in *The Dreamwork Manual* has called this technique 'Following the Dream Ego'. As with the thematic approach, you may come to realize that you are often acting in certain ways in your dreams. In Chapter 3, I referred to dream styles. I mentioned that in my dreams I often sense danger and find ways of avoiding it. Here is a not untypical dream from some time ago in which I follow the Dream Ego. I am standing by the sea shore and I sense a huge tidal wave is about to break and engulf me. I remember a technique of running towards the wave so that its full force does not break directly on me. I realize that I have only bought time and that a second wave will be coming shortly. Using the technique of following the dream ego, I ask, 'What am I doing in this dream?' I am running towards something dangerous to avoid its full impact. I am also assessing the situation and realizing that I have only managed to buy time. I do not have to work out what the tidal wave represents (although I can guess). The thematic approach would give me something similar – someone is temporarily avoiding being overwhelmed. The next step is to ask if the theme or following the dream ego in any way corresponds to everyday life. For me again the answer was yes. I can spot tricky situations very quickly and can take evasive action very readily. Often this is useful, but it sometimes means that I do not learn from situations because I anticipate difficulties which may be imaginary, and do not test my resources to the full.

Using these two techniques – the thematic approach and following the dream ego – I managed, in a very short space of time, to uncover information that was important for my everyday life. The awareness of how much my avoidance patterns dominate not only my waking life, but also my dreaming one, has led to some changes, especially in my home life.

What Am I Feeling?

A third approach, related to what am I doing in the dream, is what am I feeling in the dream? In the above dream, I am scared but not paralysed with fear. Once more, we are drawn away from meanings to looking at the quality of the dream, and seeing if this has relevance or usefulness in everyday life.

Am I Active or Passive?

A further question after what am I doing and feeling is, am I active or passive in this dream? In the dream about the tidal wave, I would say I was predominantly passive. Even though I took some action by running towards the wave, I did not deal with the problem. In this sense I was reactive rather than active. An active action would have been to face the wave and see what would happen. To me being active means making conscious decisions that deal with whatever has to be done. My experience of most people's dreams and indeed their daily lives is that they are reactive – responding automatically to a stimulus. This is especially true where feelings are concerned, and in fact this whole area could take up a chapter in itself. Reactivity (which I have equated here with passivity) can be seen in all blame statements – 'You made me angry', as opposed to the non-reactive 'I chose to be angry with you'. As a rule we do not like to take responsibility for our actions and feelings, preferring to claim that our actions are determined by outside events. This gives us the short term gains of avoiding the discomfort of facing how much choice we have, but lessens the amount of power we have available.

I have chosen to go into the question of active/passive-reactive because I believe that the reason why so many dreams are unpleasant is that we are predominantly in a reactive state during our waking lives. We look active, but do not consider how much we limit our choices by automatic responses. In the dream state, which is totally determined by ourselves, we see how much we put ourselves in the passive state – being chased, attacked, in difficult situations. I believe this reflects how we are in daily life, although we do not allow ourselves to know it.

Stripped of the necessity for action, the underlying feelings emerge. It is for this reason that working with dreams can give insights that are very practical for everyday living.

To illustrate this point further, there was a time when I was having trouble writing this book. I was not sure why I was doing it. I had been asked to do it by the publishers and it seemed too good an opportunity to miss. It was not until I could see how much I was trying to prove something to my dead father who had himself wanted to write, that I began to realize some of the internal conflicts in which I was involved. In other words, I was writing this book from a reactive state. Understanding this freed my writing.

At this point, some readers may protest that everything cannot be analysed and that there are some things for which you can't be responsible. This may be so but for me looking at dream themes enables me to assess how much I am making conscious choices in my everyday life and this awareness has proved very useful. The cross connections between the two states and the way that working with one affects the other are nicely illustrated in a recent book by Tony Crisp, *The Instant Dream Book*.[2] In this example the dreamer found himself standing outdoors in the dark. He was in a space like a park and was watching his daughter go down a slide. He didn't move, he just watched. All the dreamer's dreams were of this kind – in the dark, inactive and watching. He could see what a poor inner life he had and how this related to his outer life where he expected other people to make decisions for him. Through realizing his passivity he began to think how he could be more active in his daily life and his dreams began to change. After a while he had the following dream. 'I am in a bungalow. It is light and empty and I am decorating it, getting it ready to live in. There is some problem with the toilet and I am working at unblocking it.' The feel of this dream is totally different and reflects the changes he had begun to make in his daily life after realizing how passive he had been.

In this way, dreams can act as a progress report, a kind of mirror of the external world. The obvious question is whether by consciously trying to affect our dream worlds we can bring changes in our everyday existence. I do believe this is possible and the work with guided fantasy (like I did with Teri) certainly supports this view. I shall return to this question on page 74 when I deal with the technique of Active Imagination.

Key Questions

Following the line of looking for trends rather than meanings, I also use the dreams as a springboard for asking questions which will help expand certain aspects of the dream. I have already suggested this with such questions as, 'What am I doing?' 'What am I feeling?' 'Am I active or passive?' These are questions that can be applied to all dreams. However this technique called 'Key Questions'[3] asks questions that are specific to the dream or explore its quality. The skill is in being able to ask meaningful questions that will be useful. It is a technique that one can use on one's own, but here is an example where someone worked with one of my dreams in this way. In the dream I am talking to M, a senior staff member where I work and who I have had some difficulty getting on with in the past. I am saying that I am very good at being intuitive, taking the big intuitive steps, but not so good at the little ones. I see my brother-in-law in the background and give him a big hug. I couldn't initially make too much of the dream, but using these key questions clarified it greatly. Here are some of them in relation to my dream which will give you some idea of the technique:

1. What does missing steps in between mean for me a) in the dream, b) in everyday life?
2. How did M. feel and respond?
3. What are my brother-in-law's qualities that I would like to embrace?
4. How did I feel about what I said to M?
5. Why am I having this conversation with her?
6. Is there a huge step I need to take in my life at the moment?

Through the questions, I was able to realize that M and my brother-in-law have both taken big commitment steps –

one in becoming head of the department, the other in getting married and starting a home. Both have encountered the nitty-gritty of life which taking on responsibility entails, and which, up to now, I have mostly avoided. However, embracing my brother-in-law and talking to M seemed to indicate that I was ready to approach the question of commitment and responsibility. Working with the dream gave me the extra push and speeded up a process that was beginning to happen anyway.

As a further guide to Key Questions, I would like to refer you to the work of Calvin Hall.[4] He studied thousands of dreams and came to the conclusion that, by and large, dreams dealt with the following issues. First, *how do I see myself?* In dreams we often see ourselves as we actually are, not as the image we often portray. The next question is *how do I see others?* Are they helpful, friendly, aggressive, for example? The third question is *how do I see the world?* Is it a dangerous place full of obstacles, or a place to learn? The fourth question is *how do I see my impulses* such as sex and aggression? How good am I at gratifying my wishes or do I sabotage myself? What inner laws do I have? These can be seen operating very clearly in dreams. For example, in one dream I was settling down very nicely to have an amorous embrace with someone when I heard someone come up the stairs. In the dream I laughed because I realized that I had created the obstacle myself.

The fifth and final question that Hall thought was dealt with in dreams is *how do I see my conflicts?* Hall saw five main types of conflict. First, love and hate in the parent/child relationship. Our early relationships with our parents affect us for the rest of our lives, and these will come out in dreams involving childhood scenes or people with whom we now have dependency/authority relationships, such as bosses or teachers. The second basic conflict is freedom versus security – the need to be free conflicting with the need to belong, with the restrictions that belonging incurs. The third conflict is between masculinity and femininity. We all have both masculine and feminine parts in us, although these may be repressed for fear of being like the opposite sex. Accordingly this conflict may come up in dreams. The fourth conflict is right versus wrong. In Freudian terms this could be seen as conflict between the id and the superego – our impulses and the demands of our conscience. The final conflict is between life and death; in Freudian terms between Eros and Thanatos. So, in addition to the five questions, Hall looked for which basic conflict the dreamer was dealing with at the time.

Dialoguing with Dream Symbols

Focusing on conflicts is an integral part of Gestalt dream work which I have already touched on when I suggested dialoguing with your dreams (see page 58). The technique of dialoguing is used with any of the symbols of the dream, including animals and inanimate objects. The theory behind this is that all parts of the dream are parts of oneself. This includes all that is frightening and repulsive as well as all that is beautiful. The idea intuitively makes sense to me. In that we create our own dreams, it seems relevant to treat all parts as belonging to us. For me the dream is often an attempt to complete a piece of unfinished business, an attempt to integrate something that has been sparked off maybe by the day's events, but also relates to earlier conflicts such as those suggested by Hall. In this way it is not enough to say I had a bad dream because of the horror movie on television last night. It becomes important to find out what part of your personality the frightening aspect represents.

The technique for dialoguing is the same as dialoguing with your dreams. It can be done in written form, but is best done with a cushion or chair. To start the dialogue with one of your dream symbols, first visualize it clearly on the cushion. Then when you are ready, you can begin with a question – for example, 'Why did you come into my dream?' Or 'What do you want from me?' Alternatively, simply start with an expression of feeling towards the part of the dream, like 'I'm really angry that you keep appearing in my dreams'. Then switch cushions. Try and suspend judgement and feel yourself into your part (anything from a window pane to a prehistoric monster). What body position feels right for that part? The more you can feel yourself into the role, the more you will allow the answers and dialogues to emerge rather than having to think them out yourself. When you have replied as part of the dream, you can switch places and answer as yourself.

Working like this allows the symbols to speak and you don't have to guess at their meaning. What comes out will often be very surprising – for example, something that may have terrified you in your dreams, when given a voice says that it is only trying to reach you. Having done hundreds of these dialogues with myself and others, I can testify that they are often very illuminating. No amount of conscious effort to work out what the symbols mean can replace actually giving them a voice. In the dialogue a conflict between two parts of yourself may emerge. In Gestalt terms these often emerge as topdog and underdog – the former using words like 'should' and 'ought' and sounding quite parental, moralistic and authoritarian, the latter apologizing, whining, making excuses or being defiant in a victim way. Aim to integrate polarities and find out what each side needs.

Much of this dialogue work was done by the founder of Gestalt therapy, Fritz Perls, [5] in groups. It certainly helps to have someone else there to maintain the flow of dialogue, but it is possible to keep it going on your own. In choosing the symbol to start dialoguing with, it is often good to start with the one with most energy in the dream, although I have seen striking results emerge from what have initially seemed like unimportant symbols. A member of a dream group recently presented a long dream and during the second telling mentioned that it had been raining. When asked to choose what caught his attention, he said the rain. This became a symbol for father and then God in one dialogue (it was both intruding and nourishing) so find out in your dialogue what each part wants and needs. This may be the first time that a repressed part of your personality has had the chance to speak, so listen carefully. The aim is always to get to know the various parts thoroughly and work towards integration, accepting them as parts of yourself which have needs and may be in conflict with other parts.

If you do not want to dialogue with empty chairs or cushions, it is possible to do it in writing. You may like to try writing as fast as you can to bypass the part of you that censors. When the writing dwindles to a halt or does not seem to be getting anywhere, I try and trick myself with a question such as, 'What I don't want to know about is . . .' I then find out a little more about any blocks and resistances, and this helps me to continue. On one occasion I freed myself to continue writing for pages with one particular symbol. It was a very moving experience for me, and the symbol came alive and went far beyond anything I could have consciously imagined. It was especially good for me because I thought I had understood what the symbol meant. At the end of the dialogue try re-reading it. Is there anything more you need, like making a decision or talking anything over with anyone?

The power of such a technique rests in helping us to reintegrate parts of ourselves that are disowned or that we are unaware of. This is especially useful for nightmares, where talking to and becoming the frightening parts lessens the fear greatly. We project parts of ourselves we do not like on to others – whether other races, countries, strangers or nightmare figures. Recognizing that we have these qualities leads to wholeness.

The other reason why I think the dialoguing technique is so powerful is that it provides an opportunity for experiencing rather than interpreting. As a result of this, insight and feelings come from a much deeper level. Here is a simple dream to illustrate this difference. I dreamt that W, an ex-resident from an after-care hostel where I used to work, was standing in the street looking forlorn. Interpreting the dream was easy. He was a part of me that I had neglected. However when I became him in his loneliness I really felt that part of me and tears poured down my cheeks. Knowing intellectually and experiencing were quite different. The experience was so strong that I could hardly distinguish between the two of us and a larger part of me wanted to rush out and find him, i.e. it was such a difficult part of me to integrate that I still wanted to keep it external.

One of the criticisms of Gestalt dreamwork is that it can fragment the dream by isolating the parts of it, thereby taking you away from the dream as a whole. In much of Gestalt dreamwork the dream is a departure point from which the dreamer can find out about underlying conflicts by taking on different roles from the dream. By having a dialogue between two parts of the dream, the part they play in the dream as a whole can be lost. This drawback can be overcome by returning to the whole dream after going through the whole Gestalt process.

There are also dreams where I would not initially use Gestalt techniques – particularly so called 'big' dreams which may involve some kind of religious or mystical experience. Later it may be relevant to ask the person to become part of the dream but initially it is usually more important to acknowledge the profound impact of the dream on the dreamer.

Writing the dream as if one of the characters
Another possibility is writing the dream from the point of view of one of the symbols or characters involved. This is slightly different from becoming the character in that it involves staying with the dream and describing it from that character's point of view. This can then be a useful way into your dialogue.

Free Association
This technique involves taking a symbol or character and asking yourself what comes to mind when you think of it. Try and catch the first thing no matter how unrelated it appears. For example, in Joan's dream (page 32) I asked her what her association to X was and she replied that she had remarried. This gave a clue to the whole dream although as I explained it was not sufficient to just go for meaning. Similarly in a recent dream I was asked to do some singing which I was unable to do. In the end I settled for playing a washboard and fooling around with it as a compromise. Joan asked me to associate to the washboard and I thought of her ex-husband who used to play in a rock band. What seemed a strange dream suddenly made sense

– I was still struggling to accept that I was not Joan's first partner. However taking up the issue represented by the washboard was a safer option than that represented by the singing which I have not yet associated to – the first insight was more than enough. Actually now I am writing about it I do know. Singing represents making a stand and declaring myself to the world. I have always been afraid to sing, believing I have a very flat voice, but also knowing at some level that everyone can sing if they let go. So I am evading declaring myself fully by hiding behind the relationship issue. Just knowing this is not enough for me. I need to ask myself why I had this dream at that particular moment and how I can integrate this understanding into my relationship with Joan. In more Freudian terms, I would also recognize that her ex-husband represents some aspect of my relationship with my father, who had a relationship with my mother before I did so that the associations go well beyond the dream into childhood relationships. In fact having had the dream last night I am quite overwhelmed by the different levels.

If you are keeping a diary, you might like to include a list of symbols and your associations to them after each dream, along with titles, 'What am I doing and feeling', 'Am I active or passive' and any dialogues. Don't feel you have to use every technique. My purpose in describing them is to make them available resources.

Continuing the Dream: Active Imagination

You will probably have noticed that more often than not you awake from a dream with a feeling of incompleteness. Sometimes it is a nightmare that you have woken yourself up from in fear. Sometimes you wake up without the dream reaching any resolution or with a feeling that it is tailing off into nowhere. Sometimes, I wake myself up because I start to enjoy myself. I have a strong superego in my dreams. It is rare to have a dream that stands by itself – that needs no working on like some of the creative dreams described earlier. After many unfinished dreams unresolved feelings may carry over into the day.

One technique I use for such dreams is continuing the

dream. This is especially useful with nightmares, but can be used for all dreams. Working in this way offers the opportunity to re-experience the dream and continue at the point where it was left off for whatever reason – pleasure or fear. By consciously facing whatever could not be faced, the personality has the chance to grow and integrate what has been previously unbearable material.

For some people, doing this can be quite frightening. If this is so, you may like to write out the continuation. To do this you will have to let yourself go back into the dream state and then allow the images to develop and unfold. Writing, as opposed to lying down and closing your eyes, will help stop you from being overwhelmed. As additional guidelines, remember that the rules for imagination/dreams are not the same as for life. If you are run over in a dream, you will not die. If a masked man is coming towards you in real life, the best course of action is probably to run. In a dream this action is probably totally inappropriate. Look carefully at the danger, knowing that it cannot harm you. Ask it what it wants, who it is. Or maybe let it do what it wants and see what happens. Allow the story to develop as much as you can.

The other alternative is to lie down and relax as much as possible with your eyes closed and then continue the dream in this position. I used this method with Teri (described in Chapter 4) when she could not remember a dream. Once she had an image, I encouraged her to let the story continue. An outside person is often very useful, but not necessary.

The advantage of working like this is that you can create new possibilities for yourself. In one example, the dreamer was always struggling in a race and even in his continuation of the dream, he could not free himself from the struggle. Finally after several attempts, he realized that he did not have to be in a race and could enjoy the sensation of running. On another level this was a metaphor for his life. He had tried different ways of surviving in a highly competitive field, but they had always involved staying in the field. Little wonder he could not imagine other ways of finishing the dream, and that he was always stuck. When he finally realized he did not have to be racing, he was able to take this insight to his outer world, leave the field of work and enjoy his talents in a different way.

Finishing the dream does not mean creating a happy ending without dealing with the issues involved. Beware of coming to an end too quickly, creating your own end rather than letting the ending come from your imagination. This balance between staying in control and not being overwhelmed, and allowing the work to come from your unconscious is difficult to achieve. A check is to see if what comes up surprises you. If it is something you already knew, the chances are you are still controlling the continuation of the dream.

Transforming at such a deep level will have repercussions for everyday life. In fact for dreamwork to be really valuable, it may be useful to ask yourself what action you can take with this insight/experience/resolution of conflict. Although I believe that just working with dreams will have a productive effect, there is still a danger of stopping short of taking the results into everyday life. When I was involved in groupwork in the early seventies, it became easy to recognise the 'groupies' – people who would come for the experience or the high and still be working on the same issues time after time. Having said that, I would like to add that I do not see dreamwork as being only part of the Change/Self Improvement ethic. There is a danger in using dreams to bolster one's ego, avoid conscious responsibility by handing it over to the dream, or to drive oneself into an 'ought' situation. Although I believe dreamwork can, and does, change lives by acting as some kind of rehearsal and portrayal of the internal conflicts which we later externalize onto the world, I would hope it is approached with curiosity and pleasure rather than ego aggrandizement.

Lucid Dreams
This state is the awareness that you are dreaming in your dream. Many books extol the virtues of such a state, encouraging you to have lucid dreams in which you can fly, have orgasms and do anything you like. The main

advantage as far as I can see (orgasms notwithstanding) is help with nightmares. A tribe called the Senoi are believed to have trained their children to cope with nightmares. From a very early age children who had bad dreams were encouraged to face the danger in their dream state either by confronting the frightening image or by making friends with it. The technique was used by a patient of a friend of mine who had been told about lucid dreaming. In a recurrent dream about arriving home after his mother died, he remembered the advice of his therapist to do it differently. In the next dream he arrived in time to tell her that he loved her. He was not disturbed by the dream again. Moreover he was able to be more open with his mother in his waking life and let go of his none-too-healthy attachment to her. This technique can be used with children – telling them to make friends with the monster or imagine that one of the parents is there with them. There is less of a distinction between dreaming and waking for children, so they can easily carry over such suggestions into their dreams.

Painting or Dancing the Dream
In an earlier chapter I mentioned that one of the difficulties of remembering dreams is translating them into linear structures using words, when the dream itself is visual and not necessarily following the same rules of time and space. An alternative or addition to writing dreams down is to paint them, sculpt or dance them, write a poem or mime them out.

Dream Incubation
Finally I would like to mention the technique of dream incubation. This ancient art involves preparing yourself for sleep in order to have a certain kind of dream. It was used extensively in Ancient Greece where pilgrims would visit the temple at Epidaurus for healing dreams. The preparations included fasting and certain rituals. These techniques are also used by American Indians to get 'big' dreams. How I use this technique is to write about a problem I would like help with just before going to bed. I

deal with all the relevant issues I can consciously think of – how long I have had it, what I have tried to do about it, my investment in having it, how I feel about it, and what I hope to gain from solving it. I then ask for a dream that will give a representation of the problem. I do not ask for a solution, as I think it is the waking me that must decide. This method has been described extensively in Gayle Delaney's book *Living Your Dreams*.[6] My only reservation is the trivializing aspect that can easily develop – such as asking dreams what I should wear for tomorrow's party. I therefore encourage people to use incubation sparingly and with some humility, and to be patient in waiting for their answers.

This list of techniques has been brief and I have indicated the source so that readers can take them further if they wish. The idea is to take what works for you. The focus of this book, however, is sharing. I decided to go into detail about ways of working on your own because this is how I first came to dreamwork. Mastering these techniques on my own gave me the confidence to work with others. Ultimately, it is the social aspect of dreaming that has interested me the most, sharing with friends and my partner, starting groups and culminating in the social act of writing this book.

6.

WHY SHARING?

'It may be that healing lies in the sharing of the dream with another person, rather than its interpretation.'

Bernard Steinzor[1]

'We suggest that the missing component is not some understanding of dreams but more sharing and living of dreams.'

Corriere et al[2]

'Respect your brother's dreams.'

Native American proverb

Some years ago, a client of mine who had been quite hostile to me for most of her time in therapy, told me a very short dream. She dreamt that I had planned to take her to Kensington Gardens and she awoke with great joy. It was the fact that I had planned to take her there which had caused her the joy – that I had been so attentive. This simple dream was told to me with considerable embarrassment and, I think, courage. She was in fact saying to me, 'Can I trust you enough to tell you how important you are to me, something I have up to now hidden with my hostility?' We both knew it was not only the dream, but her willingness to share it with me that was a turning point in our relationship.

Both Jung and Freud have helped bring back the idea that dreams are worthy of attention, but the sharing they have encouraged has been within the confines of the

consulting room. As with the client above, this in itself can
be a very moving and significant occasion, but need not be
limited to therapeutic encounters.

The significance of some of the most famous of all
dreams in the Bible – for example the dream of Joseph in
which the sheaves of corn and the sun, moon and stars
bowed to him – depended on their being shared, for it was
this that drew his brothers' wrath and caused the chain of
events that led Joseph to Egypt. It was the shared dreams
of the butler and the baker, successfully interpreted, that
were instrumental in freeing Joseph from prison, and
Pharoah's dreams, when shared and acted on, saved Egypt
from famine. We do not have to look to the Bible for
dreams that have been shared. Every dream that is not
your own, whether you have read it in a book, magazine or
newspaper column, or heard it from a friend, stranger or
partner is an example of a shared dream. In fact dream
sharing of some sort or another may be more common
than is generally realized. In describing the different ways
of sharing, however, I will be suggesting that most can be
gained from face-to-face regular sharing with people you
know well. In this way the dreams can become part of
everyday living and the deepening of relationships.

Comparisons with other civilizations and cultures, unless
very well researched, tend to highlight material that suits
the argument that one is putting forward. I would,
however, like to tell you the story of the Senoi, a non-
literate people who live in the jungles of the Malay
peninsula. What has made them a focus of considerable
interest to me and others is their ways of sharing dreams
and the impact that has had on their culture. I deliberately
tell it as a story both because recent evidence has thrown
considerable doubt on the authenticity of original accounts,
and because I think cross-cultural comparisons can be
very misleading. However, the Senoi myth has been a
source of inspiration to many dreamworkers and certainly
inspired me when I first moved from working on my own
dreams to working with others'.

The Senoi were first 'discovered' by a British anthro-
pologist named Herbert Noone. He was joined in the 1930s

by a psychologist, Kilton Stewart. Noone was killed in the Second World War and the notes he made on the Senoi were buried and not found, so that all that remains are Kilton Stewart's accounts. In these (*Dream Theory in Malaya*[3] and *Mental Hygiene and World Peace*) he described the Senoi as not having had a violent crime for two or three hundred years, as being a peace-loving tribe with no need of police force, jail or psychiatric hospital, and having a society run on democratic lines. He attributed this to their methods of dream interpretation and expression which are a feature of child education and common knowledge to all Senoi adults.

His descriptions of how the Senoi deal with certain kinds of dreams have been written about elsewhere (particularly Patricia Garfield's *Creative Dreaming*, which has a section on dealing with nightmares, based on Senoi techniques[4]). However the dream techniques were not done in isolation but formed part of the community structure. This community structure is described in Corriere *et al Dreaming and Waking*.[5] In a typical settlement, there was one long house which provided a place for ceremonial activitities. This was supplemented by smaller dwelling units which contained a small extended or nuclear family. The authors of *Dreaming and Waking* say, 'Every structure enhanced the strong sense of belonging to the community. Both time and space were carefully reserved for sharing. This mundane fact can be passed over as some form of primitivism, yet it was the basis of a powerful system of psychology that worked. Who would argue with the fact of the failure of our own private society to provide such a system? Since we have so little time and few places for communing in our society, we go outside our community for this sharing, usually to an office of a strange shaman.' In fact I do not totally agree with them as in recent years there has been a rise in self help groups, especially through the Women's Movement. However, by and large it is external agencies that do our law keeping, caring, and healing.

In the Senoi system of sharing, everyone meets in the morning to share dreams. The child is educated from an early age about the importance of his or her dreams. 'The child is impressed by the fact that the adults do listen to his dreams and take them seriously, that they do trace them back to shocks, accidents and conflicts of the day before, and that they do often modify their behaviour and ask others to do so, on the basis of the data that the dream presents.'[6] In this way the dream becomes part of the relationships with the community, all the more so because the dreams are shared in the community. As Corriere *et al* say, 'It is not the dreams that made Senoi psychology unique, but the community that supported the dream. Perhaps the greatest psychological technique developed by the Senoi was the daily time set aside for communing . . . Psychoanalysis is not a way of life. The Senoi dream interpretation was, because the community did not just interpret, but interacted with the dreamer.'[7]

Whether the story of the Senoi be true or not (certainly recent research[8] has cast doubt on Stewart's work and its subsequent popularization by Patricia Garfield), the communal nature of dream sharing is a vision which appeals to me and many others who work with dreams. Although most quoted, the Senoi are not the only ones who have worked with dreams communally. Many North American Indians used the dream as part of their communal living. A dreamer was expected to share any songs, dances or visions that might be of benefit to the tribe and the community would rally round the dreamer if it seemed from his dream that he needed some kind of healing. In this way the community is as important for the dreamer as the dreams are for the community. Describing the Iroquois Corriere says, 'Dreams are not to brood over, to analyse, or to prompt lonely and independent action; they are to be told, or at least hinted at, and it is for other people to be active. The community rallies round the dream with gifts and ritual'.[9]

In their description of dream communities Corriere *et al* say, 'It is the attitude of making the private public which is the feature of dream communities'. There is always a danger of retreating into the noble savage myth (Senoi good, us bad, they simple, we complex). But the increase in individualism which the West has given us, while allowing us more freedom to do our own thing, seems to have also increased isolation and loneliness. In psychological terms, it may have *lessened* individual freedom, as one result of the increased freedom and mobility is the difficulty of sharing internal events except with a paid professional who we do not see in other contexts. The point is relevant not only to dream sharing, but the need for closer kinds of contact in other areas. In fact the growing number of self help and neighbourhood groups is, I think, an attempt amongst other things to redress the difficulty of bringing aspects of our inner worlds to others who are not in our immediate circle.

Media Culture Versus Contact Culture

Describing how it is *internal* events that connect people with one another, Corriere argues how technology comes between people. They maintain that a media technology develops in order to remove the immediacy of moment to moment contact. They say, 'We have technological knowledge of the outer world, but very little knowledge of the inner world, and consequently very little communicating. Communicating and community depend on person to person exchanges. Today, most children grow up in a *media* dominant culture, not a *contact* dominant culture'.

They define a media culture as one in which the listener's or viewer's responses do not immediately affect the message of the sender. In contact culture, on the other hand, people affect each other directly by their exchanges. 'Only in a contact culture can feelings be shown; a media culture can evoke feelings but there is no way to share and change them.'[10]

What I found especially interesting is that they argue that because of the loss of feeling function, a person reared in a media culture finds making the private public both frightening and strange. The media person will mistake the communication of facts about someone for expression of feelings for someone. Such a person will believe he knows someone when he merely knows about him. They go on to say that the desire for privacy is one of the biggest barriers to helping dreams be integrated and have a changing effect (they call this transformative dreaming). They say media dependent people do not have inner reality or outer community to support this transformative dreaming.

A while ago I visited a man who writes a dream column for a national daily newspaper. He has literally hundreds of letters and he showed me some of them. They were very moving – dreams people had had as much as twenty years previously, or even more; childhood dreams, recurrent nightmares which were causing considerable distress, religious and spiritual dreams. A few of these were answered in the columns of the newspaper, but even these had to fit into a certain length and were obviously chosen for readability. There was no come-back as to how useful the answers were. The majority of dreamers received no feedback whatsoever. Now the man who wrote this column is I think a person of great integrity, but although I can see how he hoped to promote interest in dreams by his column, I still see him as to some extent colluding with the media culture by not being able to answer people personally, and by interpreting the dreams he did without meeting the dreamer. (This is not the only way he works with dreams and I can vouch for the depth of his work with dreams in general. The point I am making is that although he has reached many people with his column, the contact, inevitably, is not there.) This meant that however accurate the interpretation, it could only reach one level and, as we have seen, dreams can operate on many levels at once. These can usually only be made clear by talking to the dreamer and gathering associations. On the other hand, in sharing and working on dreams face-to-face. we experience not only the value of the interpretation but the links the sharing makes between the dreamers.

Corriere *et al's* book on dream communities is, as far as I know, one of the few modern books which emphasizes community and sharing in working with dreams. In spite of this emphasis, however, the authors' guidelines are mostly for the individual dreamer with advice on how to make dreams more effective. So although they describe a modern dream community (their own) and other communities, their practical advice mostly stresses ways of getting the transformative dream they consider best rather than giving guidelines for setting up different ways of sharing.

Advantages of Sharing

My belief in the value of making what is private public and sharing internal events formed the basis of my work as a practitioner in a therapeutic community. The emphasis on sharing internal events made the community very successful. To finish the quote from Bernard Steinzor at the beginning of the chapter, 'In my view the encouragement to reveal oneself through all means, including dreams, is the healing force'.[11] However, even in the therapeutic community where we were doing this regularly, the dream group I started was an important extra focus for the community.

There are many advantages in sharing dreams. First is that we all have our blind spots, parts of us that we do not want to acknowledge. Others will help us to acknowledge these shadow parts that often appear in dreams, perhaps identifying with us. This can be very reassuring. Sometimes it may not be a blind spot but a part we have hidden from others. Taking the risk and sharing it can be a big relief. Second, the combined knowledge of others can throw light on some of the symbols. Recently in a group a woman shared a dream in which she had had a baby and was trying in vain to get her husband and son to look after it. Eventually she put it on the mantelpiece where it flopped over. The group looked at her needs and the way that they were not being met by her son and husband, dealing with male/female stereotypes where the woman caters for the man. However this did not seem to be getting very far. The night before I had been reading Freud and was particularly tuned in to any sexual references. I picked up on the word 'flopped' and hazarded a guess that it was the sexual side of the relationship which was suffering most. This was, in fact, the case and opened up an area the woman had been wanting to share with the group for ages.

The third advantage is that the group can provide safety and support. What turns out to be a very scary feeling – say wanting to murder someone – will probably have been experienced by others in the group. Finally we learn from other people's dreams and their insights. At one level we all have similar issues which dreams tend to touch on, such as birth, death, sex, conflict, love and although there are obviously great individual differences in dreams, there is also much in common. In one very moving example a woman, who belonged to a support group for home helps which had been unable to progress, shared a dream in which a baby fish in a tank died. A member of the group listening asked her about a baby dying, and the dreamer burst into tears and shared about a recent abortion. The people in the group were very supportive and shared their experiences of abortions, miscarriages and loss of babies. They started to work on a new level through the sharing of the dream and their common experience of loss.

Here is an account of one of the students I teach who came to one of my dream groups. In his account he relates the benefit of working with his own dreams and sharing them in a group.

'Before I joined a dream group I rarely recalled dreams (two or three a year) and then only in fleeting fragments that made no sense at all. I was curious to see if I could learn to recall dreams and then make sense of them. It was also true to say that because I was naive in my experience of dreams, I found other people's accounts difficult to take seriously. The first dream I recalled and analysed were basically about me and my parents, me and my own family, how I deal with anger and my anxiety about the future. If I now look over my dreams I've recorded they fall into the following major themes:

1. The need to express feelings.
2. The need to accept that feelings are not either hidden/ explosive but subtle.
3. The need to form ties with others for support.
3. The need to be closer to my wife and children.
5. The need to come to terms with how my parents have/do treat me.

6. The need to come to terms with my present attitude to work.

As a result of dreamwork I would say the following changes are taking place.

1. I am sensitised more to making sure I try and explore my feelings to others. I am learning to show what I feel. In particular I am moving away from the dichotomy of feelings being either held in or explosive.
2. I am more willing to accept help from others – this means admitting my failures and asking for help – not easy for me.
3. I feel (and so does my wife) that I am closer and more involved with my family. I spend more time with all of them and enjoy playing with them.
4. I accept my parents and how they are, but have not moved in this area.
5. I have realized my attitudes to work are subsumed under such headings as looking after myself, self assertion. As a result I am actively working on changing my behaviour and feeling better.

The dream group was a support by believing in the validity of sharing dreams and by encouraging me to go further in a safe place. I got a lot from the times I shared a dream – the telling brought back the power of the dream in a way that working alone seems not to. Other people's responses allowed me to stay with parts I found confusing or unpleasant.

At first telling dreams to other people can feel very self exposing. However much of the value in doing this lies in taking the risk and finding yourself more readily accepted by others than you expected. In later chapters I will be giving plenty of examples of dream sharing situations and how to set up your own group, but for the moment if you are keen, you could start with a friend, partner or member of your family. At first you could just listen to each other. Then you could have the other person repeat your dream back to you and then swop round. Hearing your dream aloud is more important than every detail being accurate.

Do not underestimate these simple ways of sharing.

Simply hearing yourself talk may be enough to throw light
on a dream. Recently I had a dream in which I was at an
American military station. A missile fell from the sky and
landed nearby. I was surprised that the Americans were
not too bothered. However another one landed nearby and
the Americans were in consternation. Apparently one on
its own was not dangerous, but two could interact with
some kind of chemical fusion which would be dangerous.
As soon as I told the dream, I laughed, realizing that I was
expressing my anxieties about having a baby (two people
interacting with some kind of fusion).

Again on a very simple level, there is a good example in
Tony Crisp's *The Instant Dream Book*.[12] He quotes a
woman who had a recurring nightmare from early childhood. In it she dreamt of the same place, a street with
railings she had known in childhood, and she would wake
up terrified. Forty years or so later, she told her sister
about the dream. Her sister told her that when she was five
some older boys had chased them both down that street
and were going to hit them. The sister had lied and said
that their mother was dead, and the boys had left them
alone. It was a lie, but the other sister had believed her.
After talking about this childhood experience, the nightmares ceased. Obviously not all solutions are as easy as
this, but I do believe that recurring dreams might be the
most important to share, as they come back in order that
some unfinished business be resolved.

I have been sharing dreams regularly with my partner
ever since we started to live together. This has alerted us to
each other's moods and preoccupations in the day to day
living. But it has also alerted us to deeper issues. You may
remember an earlier dream (page 32) in which Joan
dreamt that the bed was on fire from a cigarette which had
been left there. This led us to explore how although she
had consciously made the decision to live separately from
her husband, her unconscious was quite critical. As with
my dream above relating to my deep fears of having
children, we were and are able to face issues which
consciously we had not realized caused us so much
conflict.

When I was asked to write this book, I decided to try and initiate dream sharing with the whole family (myself, Joan, Ben, aged ten at the time of writing, and Joe, aged seven). No big insights or life changing experiences resulted, but it was fun gathering for the dream sharing ritual every morning and made getting ready for school, which had been a problem at the time, much easier. The idea spread to getting ready for sleep with guided fantasy and relaxation taking the place of a story for a time. The idea that sleep was a time for adventure developed. The experiment only lasted a few weeks, but a year later the children still occasionally asked for guided fantasy before going to sleep or even did it with each other. They still share their dreams when they feel like it.

Andy had been coming to one of my groups for some weeks. He had been working diligently on the self-help techniques described in the previous chapter, and from being doubtful about the value of dreams, he felt pleased with the insights that he had gained. He chose to share with us a dream that he had worked on himself, which he thought he had understood. I wondered why he was sharing it. It involved a servant down in a cellar and he said it was a part of him that he had suppressed for quite some time. I said that the insight might well be true, but would he like to dialogue with that part? As he began to get into it he began to weep softly for that child in him that the servant became, the child that he had so long repressed. The group was moved and many identified with his forgotten child. The following week Andy reported that he had been much looser with his children and had allowed himself to really enjoy them. In this case insight was not enough (as it often isn't). The re-experiencing of the servant part and the support of a group took the dream on to another level.

The power of simply sharing was shown to me on a visit to a dream sharing community in Sausalito, just outside San Francisco. This houseboat community began its dream sharing with the publication of a journal which collected dreams about the community. At the time the community was in turmoil, split in two by a development proposal

which threatened its existence and involved police, arrests
and prison for some members. The journal, called *Gates*,
became an important sharing focus for the community.
Neighbours who had not spoken to each other before,
would gather spontaneously to share dreams, especially if
they referred to the community or one another. Children
played an important part in the growth of the magazine,
persuading doubtful parents to include their dreams until
the parents became converts. The sharing of dreams
seemed to unite people on many levels.

Some of the powerful results that came from one
community sharing are described by a friend who wrote
an article in *Self and Society* (May/June 1981).[13]

Another striking discovery, when dreams are told within a
contained community, is the overlap between many of them.
I have lived in a group for some weeks, in which a Californian
Indian instituted daily dream meetings. The overlap of focus
in our dreams was exciting, even if unsurprising. What was
more uncanny was the likeness of imagery in these nocturnal
poems. And a consequence of the sharing was, for me, a shift
in consciousness, as I let myself be aware that the unconscious
mind of many other, apparently disparate people, was
probably composing my dreams as well as their own.

Sacking a staff member, going for an excursion into the
hills, and changing all our time-tables, were three of the
decisions which emerged from overlapped dreams, and
were acted on, besides many apparently dream-prompted
events affecting sub-groups and individuals. I, and I think
many there, found it easier to respect and trust dream-
messages than the apparent rationality of ordinary talk.

The often mysterious nature of dreams made everyone
give attention to each one. Its meanings, when agreed, were
to some extent internalised by everyone present. So a subtle
and thorough spiritual housekeeping was for ever in progress
in these dream-meetings, seemingly through the intuitive
faculties of everyone present. We came to know each other's
shifting needs, moods, fears and hopes through the imagery
of our dreams, which, like a certain brand of beer, reached
those parts of us that everyday talk could not.

I hope that that very brief description and reminiscence helps you see why I give special value to working on your dreams within the group where you live or work generally. For many people this is not at all practical. So much of what follows will contain the assumption that you will work in a part or a near-stranger group, and in my view much of what I might call the interactive value of your dreams will be diminished in consequence.

These kind of resonances take place with any regular sharing but I do agree with her on the value of sharing where you work or live. I would like to end with an apparently simple listening exercise which has been at the core of all my dreamsharing experiences. It can be used with anyone who tells you a dream, and I use it regularly at the beginning of any dream group I facilitate.

In this exercise I divide people into groups of three and suggest that one person tells a dream. The purpose of the exercise is not for the dreamer, but for the listeners. Their function is to notice what happens when someone tells you a dream. Do you form pictures? Do you identify with the dreamer? Are you busy trying to work out what the dream means? Do you switch off at any moment? (This can be a very important cue, perhaps indicating that you are 'blocking' or that there is something the dreamer is 'blocking' on and is skillfully leading you away.) Are you excited or bored or do you have any other feelings at any moment? What feelings do you have in your body as you listen?

I stress there are no wrong or right ways of listening, as long as you *do* listen. This exercise focuses on what happens when someone tells a dream. If you notice that you do look for meaning, that is one response, but by and large the exercise takes away the search for meaning into a wider area. Just as there are levels of dreaming, there are also levels of listening. Research in a new psychotherapy called Neuro-Linguistic Programming suggests that people process data in different ways – some visually, some auditorily, some kinaesthetically. Some people are predominantly thinkers, some intuiters, some feelers and some respond to sensation. Other than noticing what happens there are no right ways of responding. Suggesting the exercise for the benefit of the *listeners* who then feed back what happened for them, allows them to relax and not to try and *do* something with the dream. The aim is to sensitize people to *how* they listen. For what is done with a shared dream can depend at least as much on the listener as the dream. And there is nothing so intrusive as someone imposing their view on you as the truth, as opposed to sharing their personal response. The advantages of doing it in threes with two listeners, each taking it in turn to tell and listen, is that people can see how their responses were the same and where they differed. However, it is an exercise you can easily try with just one other person and will be an excellent warm-up to some of the situations of sharing in different settings described in the following chapters.

7.

SHARING DREAMS IN DIFFERENT SETTINGS

Sharing with a Partner

Many years ago I used to wake up regularly in the middle of the night and faithfully record my dreams. As part of this sublimatory activity I had an idealistic notion of having a partner with whom I would be able to share these strange dreams, with fantasies of our having telepathic dreams and shared spiritual dreams. The reality for me is a little more straightforward – Joan and I share dreams that seem to have more to do with present concerns and issues about our relationship.

The regular dream sharing nearly every morning (and sometimes in the middle of the night) has almost become underestimated by us, maybe because we do not always come to 'understand' the dreams, and are still hooked on 'meaning' despite knowing better. I sometimes wonder if it is not simply the telling of our stories and the different responses we get that are important, as we certainly do not work on every dream. Sometimes we just enjoy the stories. Somtimes we find that if we have gone to bed without resolving a row, we can still tell each other dreams in the morning. As they are on another level this allows us to switch from the groove we have got into to a level where we can make contact. Sometimes we discover that issues we thought were finished with are still around, as for example, Joan's feelings about her last marriage. She has said that it is hard for her to acknowledge to both herself and me that these feelings are still there, but it is easier when they come out in a dream. If she dreams of a boat (she and her ex-husband lived on a boat) or dreams of him directly, we usually know that something the day before, which we may have overlooked, has triggered the dream.

Dreams do not always deal with the past and many are forward-looking. In our dream sharing, the other person is usually more alert to this aspect of dreams and can give support to the one who may not have realized their anxieties about the coming day. Sometimes the dreams are not to do with the immediate concerns of the day – they are pursuing our deeper struggles. Joan's conflicts are usually over her masculine and feminine side and her fears that she will never quite make it – she is often trying to get somewhere in her dreams but obstacles are constantly getting in her way. I myself, can never quite trust that the world is really a safe place and I interrupt my dreams (even pleasurable ones) with anxieties, or resort to devious manoeuvres to avoid danger. As in dreams so in life!

Joan says, 'Despite our good intentions to the contrary, we sometimes fail to communicate and lose contact with each other. Our dreams serve, as does everything else, to keep in touch with each other, ourselves and what the hell we are doing here. To sustain a relationship, stay in contact and not lose ourselves is no easy task. For us, at least, dreams are a part of trying to do this'.

Like all dream sharing, the success of it depends on goodwill. When done in this way, the sharing can lead to better communication as each partner understands the concerns of the other – concerns that may not have been too obvious to either partner and come out as sudden withdrawal, or blaming, leaving the other partner baffled and resentful. Sharing can also increase feelings of being listened to and understood at a deep level. I know of couples who jointly do a dream incubation on some aspect of their relationship, or resolve to meet each other in their dreams. Tony Crisp describes such an example in *The Instant Dream Book*.[1] In the dream the husband is with his wife in a room which reminds him of the bedroom of the house where he lived with his first wife. His present wife asks him to move a wardrobe for her. In doing this he sees that he has damaged the top and that the wardrobe looked worn out and needed throwing away. He says, 'To me the dream suggests that I am carrying something from my first marriage into my present relationship. It felt like something shabby. When I looked at the feelings it has to do with the process of divorce. Part of me feels it is a shabby affair, something I would ideally never do. Yet I have. I don't want to go back to my early way of life, yet I am carrying the feeling of shabbiness, of second best, into my relationship. I can see I need to get rid of it'.

This theme is obviously an important one for Joan, myself and this man. I suspect that, with the marked increase in divorces, it may be an issue for many couples as ghosts from previous relationships seem to haunt present ones in a way that need not be obvious. Dream sharing is one way of working through what are inevitably difficult feelings.

With the Family

For a time our family shared dreams regularly, but now only do it occasionally; as Ben, our eldest, said, 'I'm more interested in motor bikes'. I asked Joan if she could write something for the book on our dream sharing. I had just given her a paper by an American author on controlling dreams and how to program your child to have good dreams, so her first paragraph includes some irritation at this. I have left the passage as it is, however, because I like her down to earth approach and style.

The bloody Americans have as usual got into the business of children and their dreams. Can't leave children alone – afraid of their primitive feelings so brainwash them even in their sleep. However in England we probably have the other side of the problem – the stiff upper lip syndrome – not wanting to show off or be different – so children are more likely to suppress and repress themselves and shut down on their imagination.

So, as adults, if you are interested in dreams and having your children interested in dreams, it is better if you work on your own dreams and let your children hear you do that. My children seem to like it if I tell them dreams that they have been in – not always – again they don't want unsolicited intimacies stuffed down their throats. If we are telling dreams we always do it first thing when we wake up or get up – somehow for me dreams seem to fit at that time. They are a transition from the night and being out in the world. My partner and I usually talk about how we are feeling when we get up anyway and dreams are part of this. Our youngest child will often come into our bedroom at this time and tell us a dream if he has remembered one – an enjoyable one in which he has been involved in something he likes doing.

He used to have nightmares when he was younger. The first one I remember was when he was just two. There was some monster-like figure in the corner of his room – he woke up screaming and it was difficult to get him awake enough to comfort him. It was about this time that Robin had told me about a book he had been reading where the dreamer who had a nightmare was told to go back into the dream and confront the frightening figure and ask it what it wanted. When this was done, the dreamer always found that the frightening creature became friendly and helpful to the dreamer.

It sounded a bit too good to be true, but what I liked about the idea was that it gave me something to do when Joe woke up frightened. I think one of the worst things about being a parent is having your child really upset and not being able to do anything to help – especially when it is the middle of the night and all you want to do is go back to sleep. So I told him all this and he went back to sleep and it happened just as the book said. I am not sure if he had the dream again, but he felt reassured and knows that nightmares are not anything to worry about.

Children have lots of angry feelings that they do not feel

good about, and accepting and supporting them when these feelings come out as monsters and murders in their dreams is another way of letting them know that it is OK to feel angry; and if they can be friendly towards their angry monstrous feelings, they will find a lot of support and help there.

Adults often find it useful to work on their dreams from the premise that every aspect of the dream is part of themselves. I think children understand this instinctively and do not benefit by, or wish for, explanations I also think they understand their dreams quite easily – they are not as cluttered up with judgements or as worried about their image as adults. Certainly my eldest son, who says he is not much interested in dreams has, on odd occasions, reported a dream and told us what it means. On the last occasion he was splashing around in a swimming pool in his dad's sitting room and was told to stop making a mess. He connected it with his father telling him off for making a noise while eating.

Children feel everything very strongly (so do adults but have learnt to hide this). Adults have more power than children. This means that children will often feel helpless and impotent and might not feel safe to express their feelings for fear of withdrawal of love or being punished or humiliated. As an adult I have noticed that it is easier to listen to another adult than to pay attention to what my children have to say – even if I do not mean to behave like that. And it is the same thing at school when there are so many children clamouring to be heard by one teacher. So children are left with really strong feelings they do not know what to do with, and have nightmares where these feelings are turned into scenes of horror and monsters. It is important for the child's peace of mind that his parents can accept his feelings, and validate them by listening to his nightmares. It is also important that the parents do not get frightened or feel out of control, and by doing so infer that the child's feelings are not acceptable. However, if the parent is able to accept that *they* are also angry, violent, hurt, frightened or whatever sometimes, then they will convey their own acceptance to their children.

Talking to the nightmare figures can be a way of doing this, or becoming the monster and telling the audience or himself what he is doing in the children's dream. There is a lovely

children's story where the little boy does this and the monster
gets into bed with him because he is lonely. Some children
like drawing and painting, so like to draw their dreams and
monsters or make clay models of them. Some children like to
write their dreams down – that is another way of validating
the feelings in the dream and making them everyday and
manageable. My eldest son taped one of his dreams, one that
involved him and me and was obviously very important to
him. First he told it to me, then he taped it, then he told it to
my partner. He probably gave it about half an hour's attention
in all before he felt satisfied. As I said earlier, he does not see
himself as being interested in dreams, but every now and
then makes use of our interest when something affects him.
He has probably done this four or five times, but they have all
been significant for him. I think it helps to make him more
open-minded about himself and others, less judgemental
about what is and is not OK, and more open to his imagination.

   Another thing I did to encourage familiarity with their
inner world and sharing it with others was to do some
relaxation and guided imagery. My very macho outgoing
eldest son had already showed this side of himself when he
had invited us into his room to do some dancing and he led us
through a dance when we became a seed in the soil, grew into
a plant which flowered and then died back into the soil.

   The children loved the relaxation we did. Using the
guidelines in *Mother Wit*[2] I got them to breathe deeper and
deeper, imagining blowing their breath across the world –
going through their body starting with their feet and tensing
each part of their body as tight as they could, and then
relaxing it all the way up their legs, buttocks, stomach, back,
arms, chest, neck, head and face. Then when they were fully
relaxed I would have them find a hidden door in their room
that they would go through and then down some steps or
down a slide and then off on a journey they wanted – down to
the bottom of the sea in a submarine, going to a field and
exploring the field, going up a mountain, going to an island
and meeting the natives or going swimming in the sea, going
for a ride on a magic carpet – sometimes I made up the stories,
sometimes they did – trouble was when they did the relaxation
they did it so well that I always fell asleep! They said it helped

them to have a more relaxed sleep and they found it easier to get up in the mornings for school. They were also less frenetic. They also did it with each other when I was not there which felt good, as being brothers they tend to be more into fighting contact sometimes and it was good that they enjoyed and shared this soft way of being together. I forgot to mention that they always brought themselves back out of the journey by coming back the same way as they went in. If you tell them to listen to the sound of your voice they always finish the journey when you say.

Re-opening Blocked Communication in a Family

In a paper by family therapists working in a child guidance unit, the writers explain how they use dreams as part of their work.[3] 'Families, like all institutions, will only tolerate as much expression of feeling as does not threaten familial stability and the social structure . . . Working with dreams with the consent of the family opens up channels of communication that may have been blocked by the conspiracy not to rock the boat.' For example, a child may show that old wounds, which parents would like to consider healed, are in fact still open and they cite a case of a child who kept dreaming of a dead pet which parents had hoped the child would have 'forgotten'.

In dreams we are all equal and a child who relates a dream can find that a parent has had a similar dream. In one case of a twelve year old girl with school phobia she related a nightmare which involved being chased by a man with a needle which makes you walk one step in a million years. When the dream was presented to the family, the mother spontaneously said, 'But I had dreams like that when I was a child'. The father commented, 'Well, I didn't exactly have them that way, but I also had dreams of having very heavy legs and not being able to move very fast – doesn't everyone?' The similarity of feelings in all their dreams helped the parents discuss the feelings of hopelessness they all had in common.

A dream offers the chance for a child to test out parental attitudes and receptivity to wishes without having to take full responsibility and risk rejection. It can also establish the uselessness of many hypocrisies and subterfuges. The child who dreamt explicit sexual dreams had to be acknowledged by its parents as sufficiently mature to be part of adult discussion. In another example, a much younger child dreamt that a baby robin had to watch whilst its parents stealthily dismantled the nest which showed the child's awareness of the split-up of the parents which they had tried to keep hidden. A shared dream opens up communication because it is open to many possible interpretations. In this way the complexities of the family relationships can be looked at openly either through the dream or the discussion around it.

Dream Sharing in a School Community

Whilst gathering material for this book I went into a school where one of my students taught, to do a few sessions of dream sharing with the children. What follows is an account by the student, Teri, of the sharing that took place at her school. I quote the article in full, although the content of the second paragraph has already been discussed in Chapter 4. She originally wrote it at my request for the book, but has since had it published in a magazine called *Human Potential Resources*.[1]

I have been working with a small group of adolescents within a school community for two years. Although I had a personal interest in dreams and had been keeping a dream diary for a year, it didn't occur to me to introduce dreams into the curriculum. Fairly early on, however, one of the kids related a powerful dream of killing her father which stirred enough interest for me to suggest she write it down in a dream book to which we could all contribute any dreams we wished to share. This didn't take off, but it did open the space for people to bring their dreams to the group. At first they were usually in the form of nightmares, shared when we had discussions about horror films and other things that frightened us. Later, kids gradually related dreams that revealed more difficult feelings and subjects.

At about the same time, I decided to tell the kids a dream which had quite a powerful effect on our relationship. I was then exploring dreams in a workshop at college and one week I mentioned in the workshop a disturbing blankness from the previous night: I'd just been left with a feeling of depression on waking. I was encouraged to re-enter the blankness and allow an image to emerge. What came up was a fantasy of a circus in which I played a very mournful clown whose role was to walk in circles under a ladder having cold water poured over me by one of the kids. I felt very depressed because the only options I could think of were to leave the circus or stage a dramatic revolt which would have ruined the show. On 'waking' I quickly related the image to my feelings about the school where I worked, and was shocked by this indication of such negative feelings of which I hadn't been fully conscious. I also saw a new possibility of what I could do about it – I could negotiate a new script for myself.

The following morning, I gathered together a group of the kids I work with and told them my 'dream'. They picked up my sadness and frustration without me needing to explain the images, and there followed a lively and intense discussion about how we could work better together so as to meet my needs as well as theirs. My expressing my needs seemed to help them formulate theirs. The structure we evolved for ourselves was one that was new to the school and caused great interest. Since then it has continued to evolve and we have moved on from there, but I still think of that session as being the beginning of a real and dynamic relationship between me and the kids.

Since those early days, it has become quite common for individuals to bring a particularly striking dream to me and whoever else wished to listen. Often I felt kids used dreams to tell me things about themselves which they wouldn't dare to say direct. One striking example of this was with a quite troubled and aggressive girl, who, I suspected, was quite attached to the school, although she would never have admitted it. In general, her difficulty in acknowledging her softer, vulnerable feelings constituted quite a block to her emotional growth. She related a dream she had after we had a quite nerve-wracking visit from school inspectors. She dreamt that she and a group of younger kids were taken to a cliff top by one of my colleagues. He pointed to the beach way below them and said that the sparkling objects they could see were valuable and if they could collect enough they could use the money to save the school from closing. The little ones rushed down eagerly, but when the older girl tried to descend she got scared and dizzy and couldn't move. She felt ashamed that the little kids could do it but she couldn't, even though she wanted to. I felt warmed and encouraged by this indication that she did in fact care about the school and I found it easier to cope with her agression nów that I could guess it to be based on fear and insecurity.

Interestingly, this experience was completed several months later, when this same girl joined in a dream group facilitated by Robin and myself. She retold the same dream and when Robin observed to her 'The school is obviously very important to you' she beamed and acknowledged it – a tangible measure of the huge progress she had made over the months in accepting her more vulnerable feelings.

The same phenomenon could be observed with other kids who participated in this dream group – they revealed things via dreams that they could not acknowledge or communicate directly. In one session, for instance, several dreams were shared that revealed angry aggressive feelings towards parents. When I reflected this back to them it was completely denied and yet the conversation over tea at the end of the group was dominated by tales of how powerful and cruel their parents seemed.

Another thing I noticed when we ran the dream group was the number of times kids related what they saw as 'weird' dreams. They were very concerned that those were indications that they were mad or weird themselves. I was glad of the chance of accepting their dreams as quite usual and thus rendering less horrific their secret fear of 'madness'.

Introducing a dream group into the curriculum served a very useful function of bringing the importance of dreams to the attention of the wider school community. Other kids and workers, seeing my notices on the board about when it would run, started to share with me their dreams or their inability to recall dreams. On one morning, after we had successfully gained official funding – a move which we welcomed but which introduced many unknowns into our lives – one of my

colleagues told me a dream about coming into a vast insti-
tutionalised dining room. Everyone in our school was there
eating a horrible mush and looking totally depressed. She
asked in her usual enthusiastic way what everyone was
planning to do after dinner. 'Don't be silly', came the morose
reply, 'you know we can't do anything now we're part of the
local authority'.

I commented that there were probably a lot of unvoiced
fears about the implications of our new status and we
decided to put her dream on the agenda of our weekly
meeting, which was just about to start. It felt a good way of
opening up the space for people to voice their own fears if
they wanted to. Again I was struck by how easily kids can
understand the language and symbolism of dreams – they
needed no explanation of this dream any more than they had
needed to ask why I cast myself as clown in my circus dream
or what the buckets of water represented. And they always
show great pleasure at hearing they've featured in our
dreams.

My own dreams have often been about the school, the
adults and kids I work with and I often share them with the
people concerned. This has started to be reciprocated too.
Recently one of the kids in the dream group rushed in in the
morning apologising profusely to me for last night's dream in
which she'd punched me in the face for no apparent reason.
Again, simply by accepting the dream with no censure, I hope
she felt she could accept her anger towards me or whatever I
represented in her dream.

I feel excited by the opportunity opened up by dream
sharing for kids and adults to relate on a level that goes
beyond the conscious and the intellectual. It's good to have an
area in schools where adults and kids are totally equal –
everyone, after all, is an experienced and accomplished
dreamer. I also feel excited by how much practical application
they can have beyond creating a feeling of equality and
intimacy. Several dreams have given me messages which
have influenced my actions in school. I'm coming increasingly
to respect them as saying much wiser and more honest things
than my conscious mind. Not long ago, I was discussing in
supervision a problem with one child who noisily dominated

the group. Robin, my supervisor, recommended looking at the worker group, as a problem with the kids may often simply reflect one amongst the staff.

'Who', I was asked, 'is the big mouth on the staff?' I racked my brain but honestly couldn't think of anyone I'd label in this way. That night I had a dream about one of my colleagues coming into a room where another colleague was dealing with a naughty child. She started shouting, 'Look, I told you once how to deal with this child. Don't you listen?' and took over the situation in a way which totally undermined the other worker. I woke up recognising very clearly that I did see us as having one dominant group member, although my polite, conscious mind had refused to acknowledge it. This new information enabled me to observe my group with added insight and I chose soon after to reflect my observations about the group dynamics I suspected were operating. We had a useful discussion on power in the collective.

I began to encourage dream sharing at school very much as an extension of my personal interest, and as an interesting experiment. I now feel quite sure it has a unique and valuable role to play in a school community. My new aim is to see how far young people and the adults who work with them can be encouraged to use their dreams as guides to action. My fantasy is that a school guided by dreams would be a wise and caring community indeed!

Teri's article produced quite a response from people who worked in schools and were attracted to her ideas. As well as asking her to write this article, I decided to gather more examples of dream sharing. I had already worked with friends, with Joan, started a peer group, and introduced dream sharing in the therapeutic community where I worked as well as on the counselling course where I taught. I wrote to people I knew who were involved in dream sharing and gathered some articles which I published in a journal called *Self and Society*.[5] It included excellent articles from people who worked with a group of young children, a group of teenage girls in a very deprived area of Clydebank, the boat community at Sausalito mentioned in Chapter 6, and an article which included using dreams to overcome racial prejudices for white workers involved with black children. I have since heard about dream sharing in hospitals, day centres, and in a language instruction class. I mention all these to indicate the wide opportunities for dream sharing. In all these cases, and in general, it is very important to be clear about the purpose of the sharing. In the language instruction class the dream was used as a vehicle for extending French students' knowledge of English.[6] The interest aroused by dreams was used as a means to this end, and the teacher gave very clear guidelines so that students would not expect to have their dreams explored in depth. In this case the dream sharing was more like story telling with discussions afterwards on common symbols and the 'universal language' to which Fromm has referred. This would contrast with, say, a therapy group which explored dreams as part of its work.

A friend of mine recently introduced dreams as a topic in the weekly theme group at the day centre where he works. He shared his interest in dreams and some of his experiences of being in our peer group, as well as saying a little on the meaning of dreams in general. He gave some examples from Fromm's *Forgotten Language* and the group discussed symbolic language – how it appeared in most advertisements and children's stories as well as in dreams. Connecting with the idea of universal symbols, they went on to share dreams in which some of these symbols such as water, snakes and earthquakes appeared, with some good understanding of the emotions involved in such dreams. Gradually people allowed others to make more comments on their dreams. It remained primarily a theme/discussion group but the members were quite astute in picking up each others' dreams, managing to incorporate details from the person's life history as well as events that had happened at the time of the dream. In this way, although the brief was never to work in depth, it was more than a discussion group. There was so much interest that my friend extended the group. He was particularly interested in eliciting people's creativity and encouraged people to paint symbols from their own and each others' dreams. He used dreams as a basis for storytelling – group members finishing off an unfinished dream by adding to it in turn. He also used guided fantasy as part of his second eight week block of discussions.

I have sometimes been asked whether dream sharing can be dangerous. My experience is that if the listener is clear about his own boundaries and limitations (or if it is a group situation the facilitator has communicated the purpose of the group and the level on which it will work) then there are no problems. For people who do not have clear boundaries between fantasy and reality, I choose to listen to the dream and thank them for telling me, perhaps making one or two comments about the quality of the dream as it appeared to me (e.g. you seem quite frightened in the dream). Unless I have a clear and on-going contact, going into depth can bring up too much material for them to absorb. My experience has been that sharing a dream has always intuitively brought people together in understanding each other, and the groups I have been involved in have been able to respond at the level that has felt right even with clients who may have been labelled disturbed. Simply, sharing cannot be dangerous, although it may highlight disturbances that are already there.

In this chapter my aim has been to illustrate the many possible opportunities for dream sharing. Most of my experience has been in different dream sharing groups and I will describe some of these in the next chapter.

8.

EXAMPLES OF DREAM GROUPS

Dream Groups at Conferences
My first experience of being a member of a dream group was almost ten years ago at a counselling conference. One of the workshops offered was on dreams. It was a short workshop and there was only time to work on one dream which came from a woman who dreamt that she had gone on a journey through a forest and had come to a house. She was scared, but knew that she had to go in and there sat a very old woman, her face lined and wrinkled and with such an expression on it that the dreamer could not bear to look, and woke herself up. The journey through the forest had been joyous, and her terror at confronting the old woman was quite apparent. The work on the dream was very moving and I remember sitting there with tears in my eyes, awed almost by the power of the work, as the dreamer moved past her fear and began to express her love for the old woman. It was the first time, but not the last, where I had seen that it is not only the dreamer but also others in the group who benefit from the sharing and I felt privileged to be there.

Since then I have offered dream groups at other conferences I have attended. I offer them at the beginning of the day before breakfast. My purpose is to help people with their feelings about being at the conference, and I know that doing something where I feel comfortable and confident helps me too. I explain to the group that the focus I am interested in is how people's dreams are reflecting their feelings about being at the conference. In this way I am clear about the purpose of the group and do not raise any false expectations about the depth of the work. I work in this way for a variety of reasons. One is that there is not usually a lot of time – perhaps an hour at the most – before breakfast. Secondly, the group membership will change from day to day; this is not a regular on-going group where people have come to know and trust each other well. Thirdly I have noticed that being in a strange environment such as at a conference, can be sufficiently unusual and anxiety-producing to affect people's dreams. People are sometimes not conscious of the depth of feelings aroused by being at such conferences. Although a far cry from the Senoi, such morning dream sharing will give them insights about their deeper feelings about being at the conference, and will consequently affect their involvement and participation. Here are some examples.

A friend dreams that he has a large American car which has been squashed on one side and has petrol leaking out. The car is on its last legs, although the dreamer has put a lot of time and money into it. Nearby our younger son Joe is playing. The dreamer asks Joe to call his brother, but Joe isn't interested.

After he had related the dream, I asked him for his associations. It transpired that he had felt squashed on arrival and had compensated by playing with the children. His feelings about coming to the conference were able to emerge and be accepted, as people in the group identified with him. His approach to the conference changed and he recognized how often he retreated into the child part of himself.

Working in this way, with feelings about being at the conference, is obviously dealing with the dream on one level only. I did not, for example, explore the imagery of the American car. On other levels, besides coping with difficult situations by retreating into inappropriate child behaviour, there is also the theme of disappointment about the wasted time and energy put into the car. However, sticking to the feelings about the conference with what little has emerged, I ask the dreamer how he is going to spend the day. In this example, someone who identified with him asked him if he would go to a workshop with her as she was feeling anxious.

At another group a lady cannot remember her dream but has an image of being pushed to the front of the class to volunteer. Her associations were again about being at the conference. What had happened was that at a previous conference she had had a bad experience and was not going to come to one again. However, she had been persuaded by a friend to go with her, but at the last minute this friend had backed down. The woman also had another image of being on a journey on a boat which had started off pleasantly, but had caused her anxiety. The two images combined were a very accurate description of how she felt. As well as being pushed forward against her will to come to the conference (like being pushed to volunteer in the dream) she now felt at sea, literally cut off by being at the conference. Her feelings about being at the previous conference were explored, and she and the dreamer who had felt 'crushed' on arrival resolved to spend time together. Sharing the dream was an important experience for this woman as she was at the point of going home. Large groups terrified her, reminding her of her years in a convent where she had been very unhappy.

Going through my records, I find that almost all dreams shared at the beginning of a conference relate in some way to anxieties about being there. At another conference a woman dreamt that she goes into a building where there is a cold-mannered receptionist. There are long corridors and she knocked on one of the doors along one of them. She needs a tetanus injection and the secretary spends ages looking through the records and the dreamer is left anxious and frustrated. I asked her what her associations were to a tetanus injection, and she said protection. I asked, against what, and she said against feelings about being at the conference. She had felt angry, vulnerable and lonely (long corridors) the night before.

In each of the three dreams mentioned, the dreamer is using a particular image to express a common theme. As well as the anxieties about being at the conferences (day residue), the dreamer expresses something deeply personal in his/her choice of imagery. For the most part I choose not to go into this in depth as the focus is community dreaming, but the benefits, even on the relatively simple level we worked on, were very real and obvious. The dreamers were able to express their anxieties, find that others had similar feelings, connect these feelings with other incidents in their lives (e.g. life in the convent) which they had not known were still affecting them to such an extent, and make decisions about how to spend time at the conference.

These groups are unusual in that they are of short duration and consist of people who usually do not know each other. Their strength lies in the opportunity to share dreams at the beginning of the day, integrate feelings about being at the conferences, and perhaps make decisions from what emerges. More usual is a group that meets for a longer period of time – say a weekend – or is ongoing, perhaps one evening every week. In the following example, Joan and I were lucky enough to be part of a group that met for seven days as part of a spiritual retreat. This felt a real luxury as there was plenty of time, and themes could emerge from the dreamwork that were relevant for the whole group. We were to work with two Jesuit priests and a nun as co-facilitators. The first part of the day was to be for dream sharing and the afternoon for individual inter-views for spiritual direction with the three other facilitators. At 9 p.m. every evening there was a Eucharist in the chapel for whoever wanted to attend.

Seven Day Residential Group

The group consisted of seventeen members, some Jesuit nuns and priests, and members of the local religious community. We introduced ourselves and asked them to do likewise, to say why they had come, and what their experiences were of working with dreams. It turned out that many people recorded their dreams and had been interested in them for a long time. There were also some healthy sceptics so the group had a good balance.

We started with the listening exercise described at the end of Chapter 6 and we divided the groups into threes so that everyone had a chance to share a dream, notice how they and other people listened, and begin to get to know each other. This generated a lot of energy and interest which people shared in the large group once they had done the exercise. We finished the evening by giving a brief résumé of techniques for remembering and recording dreams.

The next morning we started with an opening circle. This ritual involves everyone linking arms and saying their names and something good that has happened to them, no matter how small, since we last met. It is useful for reminding the group of each other's names, for bringing people into physical contact and for sharing simple experiences. I ask for a dream from the previous night, explaining that such dreams will reflect on us as a temporary dreaming community, as well as being relevant to the individual.

We proceed to work with two dreams using a technique I will describe more fully in the next chapter. It involves the listeners taking on the dream as their own and sharing any ideas or feelings about the dream as being their own projections, i.e. to do with themselves and not the dreamer. To help do this members are asked to share their impressions with 'If this were my dream . . .' The dreamer takes what is relevant from the sharing. I notice that everyone in the group is participating in this structure and some are sharing a lot about themselves via the dream. Both dreamers are pleased with what has emerged and the group is 'warmed up'.

There is time for one more dream before lunch, and a woman named Liz shares a dream in which she was on a beach in some sort of half light. There was a large box or small hut on the beach. Two youths aged seventeen or eighteen are there and are driving a car straight at her as she stands on the box. A friend tries to distract them but they are good at driving and difficult to avoid. She wakes up in fear.

There are many ways of working with the dream such as asking her to continue it, or becoming one of the youths. It does not feel appropriate to follow the previous technique. Time before lunch is very short, so I choose to ask her a simple question, 'what happened to you when you were about seventeen or eighteen? It turns out that two very close people died then and it was a very traumatic time for her. She thought that she had successfully shut herself off from those experiences, but her dream and further work she did in the workshop showed this was not the case, and that she had been using a lot of energy trying to keep it at the back of her mind. Happening in late adolescence, I ask her if these losses had not connected death with sexuality in her mind. She agreed saying that she was always frightened of losing someone to whom she had become close. The few minutes we have spent on the dream have had quite a powerful effect on Liz.

We end with a closing circle which involves saying something good that had happened for you in the morning, or something you have enjoyed about yourself or someone else.

The following morning a man (David) shares a dream involving a sequence of events around looking after money. David wants to go to a football match, and meets a girl who he knows but initially does not recognize because of her new hair style. She gives him permission to go to the match. He goes into the changing room, and feels something wrong with his right foot. He notices that he has lost his right shoe, but his sock is not wet even though it has been raining outside.

I ask him what part of the dream he had most energy for. His answer surprises me, as it turns out to be the rain – something he had forgotten to mention when he was first telling the dream. I ask him to talk to the rain and it transpires that the rain is God – it nourishes and can sometimes overwhelm. From the tone of voice, which sounds critical, I ask if the rain could be anyone he knew. It turns out to be his father who he had despaired of, and so he had turned to God instead. However it was clear that he could not bypass his father to get to God.

We were interested to see that our work with dreams, and that of our co-facilitators, were in agreement. All of us agreed that it was not possible to deny the earthly (father) by attempting to become spiritual.

We split into small groups for the second part of the morning to give everyone a chance to share a dream. Later Joan tells me how important it was that she clarified with one sharer what he wanted from sharing – she feels she was being tested out as the person shared a dream and then did not want to work with it. In fact the work with him did turn out well, but as so often happens some groundwork had to be done first.

The following morning Paul shares a dream which involves asking a girl who is churning butter to give him some. He cannot understand her reply. Working with the dream a conflict emerges between his rage and his need to be loved. It affects the way we work with him as he feels cheated if we offer suggestions (wanting to do it himself) and cheated if we do not. The other facilitators are present in this conflict, as is the whole group, as Paul struggles and wants to blame us. We do not come to any easy resolution – the dream seems to have left him with a response he cannot understand. Liz is obviously very affected by his work. Her rage at being abandoned surfaces and is quickly denied. I imagine from her behaviour and the dream of the two youths that she fears her own destructiveness. The theme of death is very strong for her, and it turns out that her father has had a heart attack and she feels she cannot make contact with him emotionally. One of the priests plays the role of her father, and a moving dialogue ensues. Later that day she phones her father and tells him she loves him.

The next morning begins with an announcement from one of the members, who says he has been holding back from participating because of his ambivalence about

declaring his homosexuality to the group. The group is
very supportive. We again break up into small groups as
we had spent the whole of the previous day in the large
group and people need time to share their own dreams.
The shared dreams have begun to be more explicitly
sexual and we decide to tackle the theme of sexuality. I
suggest a structure (called the fishbowl) in which one
group of people sit in the middle and talk about the issue
while the rest sit outside and listen. The two groups then
switch places. In this instance, I suggest that the groups be
made up of celibates and non-celibates. The group accepts
this suggestion. One nun in the middle comes alive and
says that celibacy is a vital issue and if you do not sort it out
it will affect everything – health, feelings and attitudes;
and that as nuns they were given very little help with it.
The celibates, especially the nuns, are very open and talk
of having to sacrifice their relationships. They seemed
clearer than we non-celibates about the role of sexuality in
their lives.

The next day Joan and I, along with the three other
facilitators, decide that it would be best for the group to
work without us in small groups of four or five. Joan and I
are leaving that day, and we want to make sure that, as the
group is continuing for another two days, the power of
dream sharing is invested in the group and not in us. The
small groups work successfully without us and members
draw upon each others' resources and skills. When they
return to the large group, we begin to say our goodbyes,
discussing the format of the next two days and the
possibility of a peer group after the retreat, as many people
feel they have picked up enough to be able to work on
without an outside facilitator. Then Deidre makes an
urgent request to share a dream. The group senses its
importance and switches flow.

In her dream she is lying on a mattress in the middle of
the floor in her room at the retreat. She can see an insect
with a long black body and folded wings and turns away,
repulsed. Then, a second insect comes along the wall with
wings open a little. Again she turns away. She then sees a
third insect above her head with its wings wide open –

they are beautiful. As she looks it rushes past the right side of her head and she wakes up.

I ask her to talk to the insect and she is very resistant. As she attempts to do this, it becomes very difficult to tell who is on the Deidre cushion and who is on the insect cushion. It is obvious to everyone except Deidre that the insect is very closely connected with her sexual self. The group does not attempt to push its insights or interpretations on to her, but remains supportive, even though both she and the group are frustrated by these events. We end with a warm closing circle.

There is no way that I can have conveyed adequately in these few pages the richness of the group. Over the few days we saw how people began to take risks with observations and intuitions that had occured to them, as well as sharing their dreams. At times the group moved as a unit as it did with Deidre, knowing how far to confront and support the person working. Sharing dreams became a vehicle for sharing themes of death, sexuality, and spirituality. With one of the priests and the nun we saw many parallels in our life and theirs. Although they were struggling in a close celibate relationship, devoted to God, our approaches seemed similar.

In describing the group in some detail, my aim has been to capture some of the flavour of being at a dream group – more specifically one facilitated by Joan and myself. We focus on current group concerns as well as the dream because we believe that bringing the work back into the group grounds it, and stops dreamwork being a flight into some etheric way of being. Although a spiritually focused group, the dreams and issues arising were of a very immediate nature.

Dream Groups on a Counselling Course
Every dream group varies according to such factors as whether it is on-going, the purpose of the group, the leader's style and the membership; so no two groups are alike. My final example is of the dream groups I have facilitated on a counselling course in South London where I have been teaching for about four years. The course is for

people who use counselling skills in their work and includes nurses, teachers, social workers, youth and community workers and other people in the 'helping' professions. The students come for one day a week for three years. At the beginning of the first year of one of the courses, I offered a four week introductory group for anyone who wanted to experience being in a dream sharing group and learn some basic techniques – a kind of 'taster' group. Jean was in one of these groups. Here is an account of events leading up to a dream she shared, and the dream itself.

> After the course I used to visit one of my favourite shops, Athena in Oxford Street where there was a print of an old lady sitting in a chair. I used to look at the print and feel sad. Then one day I realized that to me, this lady was my grandmother. This had been going on for some weeks and the realization gave me some relief from the inexplicable sadness. Soon after I had a dream. I was with other people making a film in a desert. My role was to ride a horse across some distance of desert to a building. Back at base we had the task of sorting out a young boy who had committed a crime . . . We were trying to ascertain the crime the boy had committed – it was something involving another person.

After Jean had volunteered the dream to the group, I asked her to become the boy, and asked him what crime he had committed. Jean realized that the boy was part of her, and the crime she had committed was the murder of her grandmother. What had happened was that whilst a child, Jean had visited her ageing grandmother, and whilst playing with a sachet of shampoo had inadvertantly burst it with the result that some shampoo had hit the ceiling. Her grandmother had noticed the stain and had worried that her roof was leaking. Too frightened to tell the truth, the young Jean had felt that the extra stress had caused her grandmother's death. With the acknowledgement of the guilt she had been carrying for so long, Jean was able to go through a bereavement process for her grandmother, who had been a very important figure in her childhood.

Margaret also came to these introductory groups. She shared two dreams. In the first she was sitting in a beautiful garden. Suddenly through a slit in the fence at the bottom of the garden, she saw lots of police. She ran to tell her grandmother who said they were Russians. I knew that Margaret had worked with dreams before and believed that all parts of the dream were parts of herself, so I asked her to become one of the policemen. She did this in a very half-hearted way so the work soon dwindled to a halt. With the issue still unresolved, Margaret joined another four week group and shared her second dream. In this she and a lot of other people were escaping on a train. A German soldier came with a search machine and searched her all over. Again I asked her to work with the persecuting part of the dream by becoming the soldier. Again we made little headway, and in fact Margaret saw me as persecutor for suggesting that she play such roles. I knew how strongly she identified with the victim position. She had escaped from the Germans in World War Two and could not see how victim and persecutor could be connected. However, a little later Margaret acknowledged what I had been trying to do – saying that she did not have sufficient trust in me at the time. She gradually became able to own her persecutory part (the German and the Russian) and became much less of a victim. The work with the dreams had been an important landmark, although it had not seemed like it at the time.

By the end of the first year of the course, there were enough people who had been to a four week introduction to want to have a full year of dream sharing, and seven of us formed a support group. As in any group, we had to be clear about the contract. Basically we were primarily a support group, which meant that if someone had a pressing problem they would not have to wait for a dream, but could ask the group for support. However, all things being equal, dreams were to be the primary focus.

We used a variety of techniques – Gestalt, key questions, dream incubation and taking on the dream as our own (if this were my dream . . .). The continuity enabled us to recognize quickly each others' dream styles and issues that kept reappearing. We could also set each other tasks based on the dream work and the person could report back the following week. When non-dream material was presented, we were able to work on it in the same empathic way as we worked with dreams, so the group was very supportive.

The following account of one of the members, Jane, illustrates how we combined dreams and support, and also shows the value of continuity, as there is a gap of four months between the sharing of the dream and the work we did. This work lasted less than twenty minutes, but demonstrates what far-reaching effects dreamwork can have. Rosy is her twin sister, Andy is her husband. They have two children, Adam and David.

> I dreamed that I was a demon. The world was about to disappear. There was quite a long build-up and preparation for this. It is important that I convince people, by looking in the mirror, that I am a demon; there's no-one there in the mirror. We, the demons, are the only ones who can save the mothers and babies – no men. We go along country lanes, there are power lines and grassy, high banks. We are identifying in some way who is and who is not a demon. I'm trying to convince Rosy that Andy (her husband) can't come with us, it can only be us and the two children, who look just like David and Adam. Rosy is very calm and accepting of me; I'm very definite and in a great hurry.
>
> The world blows up and we, Rosy's hand on my breast, and the two babies spin off in a cocoon-like, egg-shaped 'module', with clear plastic on the top; I can see us clearly inside. There are lots of stars and black sky.
>
> I awoke from this dream rigid with fear, reciting the Lord's Prayer, and absolutely convinced there was a demon standing at the foot of my bed. I felt a need to go to the bathroom, and it took me several minutes before I had the courage to move. I was very scared to look in the mirror as I passed it – I was sure that I wouldn't be there. Once I'd done it, I had to keep looking to be sure that I was there. I had to leave a light on. I started to shake, my skin began to crawl. After I'd written the dream down, it seemed to become even stronger, as if by the writing of it I had given it reality.

This dream and my immediate reactions to it are presented above in the way in which I wrote them that night. I dreamt this in an unknown room in a hotel in France after a very long drive and late arrival.

The dream still, after several months, has power enough to distress and disturb me. It took me a lot of courage to share it with the dream group. The motivation to do so came from the urgent feeling that I had to release the energy building within me into a safe environment. The dream's power did not seem to fade with time, but kept appearing vividly in my mind at intervals, to distress, disturb and upset my day or night.

Sharing the dream with the group was a valuable, warming and self-confirming experience. Many issues of my life had been raised by the dream; my work as an abortion counsellor, my relationship with my twin sister and her children – which seems to point to the juxtaposition of destruction and creation; my need for safety and above all, my need to get a sense of where I begin and end, a sense of my own boundaries.

For some while after this sharing, I felt a confidence and self acceptance. However, I seemed to swing violently between this and feelings of inexplicable anger, and rage, power and frustration. I had many 'crazy' thoughts. I'd be sitting on an underground train, feeling very poisonous, with multi-coloured visions of poison coming from me and burning and corroding all that it touched. The experience was both frightening and very powerful, since all these people around me were sitting innocently next to me and unaware of how close they were to burning and excruciating pain. Whilst waiting for the trains, I'd stand very close to the edge of the platform and imagine jumping just as the train came in. It would hit me and my blood wouldn't be red, but green and acid, burning through the rails.

My behaviour with friends and colleagues did not seem to me to have changed, but the feedback I had from them indicated a vast gap between how I felt I was behaving and what they felt about me. Colleagues were finding it increasingly difficult to work with me, because, they said, they didn't know how I'd be, they were frightened of my reactions, they felt I was dangerous. The more aware I became of this, the more I'd try to *behave* outwardly in an acceptable, warm and

friendly way. I'd become upset and unhappy when I found
that friends were still frightened of me. This seemed to me to
be confirmation of my 'craziness'.

My dreams, at this time, seemed to be shallow, just
snippets, tail-ends, nothing that made connections for me or
meant anything to me. For a long while I was unaware of my
dreams. I would wake up with feelings of anger and distress,
that did not seem to have a focus; again, to me, confirming my
'craziness'.

Then, in our dream support group, a woman was doing
some work, going around from person to person, making
contact with each of us. She stopped at me – said nothing. I
felt a strong need to ask her why she had done that. I was both
surprised and relieved when she stated that she had stopped
in reaction to what the woman before me had said. I was
feeling pleased and happy with her reply. I was also pleased
with myself for checking it out.

Robin, the group facilitator, then focused on me and asked
what had been behind my question. Because of the sharing of
the dream he had a sense of my underlying motivation
(hidden behind the activity of checking out), and had picked
up my distress, my feeling that I was too dangerous to be
touched by her. The woman in the group had stopped at me
for totally other reasons, but my deep and hidden feeling was
that she had done so because I was dangerous, aloof,
untouchable. Robin then made connections between that
example of my behaviour, there in the group, and the dream
that I had shared four months previously. A turmoil of
feelings arose in me, and from what had appeared to be a
minor and contained interaction, suddenly became immensely
charged and powerful. I shared my feelings of power and
rage, my 'crazy' thoughts and fantasies of being dangerous
and corrosive, and my feelings of confusion and distress. This
sharing was very important for me, since my friends in the
group showed care and concern for me, and did not confirm
my 'craziness', but rather accepted it as, in some way, a
manifestation of my sense of isolation. Robin, then, referring
to the dream, and the strong image of the mirror and the
absence of my reflection in it, gave me the information that a
baby first sees herself reflected in her mother's eyes. It took

me a few moments to realize what he was saying – that my mother had not really seen me and that therefore I had little sense of myself as important and valued, as I understood, it resonated so deeply within that I could not reply, but shook both physically and emotionally.

I took this information and realization home with me. I thought of it, it cropped up suddenly in my mind and my gut at odd moments, it was with me and accessible to me at any moment. Robin had suggested at the end of the group that I ask my dreams to show me a way of descending into this area of my life safely. This I did and from that night on my dreams, previously unremembered, were vivid, full of imagery that held much for me. Over the next few weeks I looked forward with excitement to the night and my dreams, wondering what they would show me, what emotions I would experience there. I became quite used to waking and spending some time at four or five a.m. writing my dreams down. A few moments of wakefulness seemed a small price to pay for the relief I felt in dreaming. They became a place in which I could give vent to my anger and frustration and experience my power safely. The 'work' which I had done in the dream group seemed to have released this energy in dreams. This work has given me a framework, a base, from which I can experience my 'craziness' safely, and not feel it as crazy at all, but as an exploration, within my dreams, of my boundaries, of my power, of my anger. By having my 'crazy' image of myself as a demon, with no reflection in a mirror, based in a reality which I feel strongly to be true for me, I was given permission to dream, to experience myself in my dreams, to use my dreams to test out my boundaries.

This has spilled over into my waking life, where my behaviour at work has become more 'congruent', my friends and colleagues seem less frightened and wary of me. I feel more certain of my limits, and can relate more realistically to those around me.

I don't expect that the sort of power that the images in my dream hold, nor the realization of where they originated for me, or the implications that they have for me, have gone forever. I suspect that I have a lot more work to do, and that from time to time I shall again be overwhelmed by my 'craziness'. However I feel that through my experiences within the dream group I have begun to work on myself at a level I would have found more difficult or impossible to reach in other ways. The sharing and subsequent work I did on my dream within the dream support group has been an exciting, frustrating and rewarding process.

After two years there was a strong culture of dream sharing on the course. About this time one of the staff members lost a six-weeks-old baby through a cot death. It was difficult for us all individually and as a group to come to terms with the loss, and to know how to approach the mother. One way was through dreams, people going up and telling her of dreams in which she had appeared or in which they had told her that they cared about her. The staff member experienced the goodwill in the sharing and that people were thinking of her. In my case I had a dream in which I was trying to steal something to give to her which she refused, and we discussed my primitive need to make reparation. On another level dreams are usually about parts of ourselves and we all knew this. But somehow just dealing with them on this social level seemed healing.

In the third and final year, the harsh realities of assessment seemed to take precedence over all else* and I and others succumbed to cultural norms by not giving dreams a place on the timetable**. I was sad that when the pressure was on, we once more became 'practical'. I too was part of this process, and wonder if what turned out for many to have been a very fraught third year – with feelings of competition, fear of failure and of being judged – might not have been made easier by the co-operation and identification that had come from the dream sharing of the previous two years.

---

*The course is self directing, and in the final year the students assess each other and award diplomas or not as the case may be.
**There is also no set syllabus, and the timetable is co-operatively worked out by the whole community.

9.

WORKING IN A GROUP – GROUP DYNAMICS AND TECHNIQUES

GROUP DYNAMICS

Dreams as Forms of Communication

Through my work with dream groups over many years, I have come to believe that all dreams shared in a group are saying something about the dreamer's relationship with the group, and are not just about the dream. Even if the dream was dreamt before the dreamer belonged to the dream group, the sharing of the dream is a message to the group. It may be saying, 'I trust you with this important dream', or 'Look what special dreams I have' or 'I'll test you out with an old dream before I tell you a current one'.

However current dreams usually have even more direct messages. They will have been dreamt when the dreamer knows that he is going to a dream group, so not only the telling of the dream, but also the content of it will often relate directly to the group. It is as if sometimes the dream has been dreamt for the group. (This idea is not new and forms the basis of much psychoanalytic dream interpretation where the dream is seen as a message to the analyst.) This need not only be true for groups. At the beginning of Chapter 6, I related the dream of a client who dreamt that I

had planned to take her to Kensington Gardens. This was a
very direct message to me. Sometimes the messages will
be more coded.

On one particular residential weekend group which ran
from Friday night to Sunday, Joan and I, although the
facilitators, were by far the youngest people there. The
group was taking place in a residential retreat, often used
by spiritually inclined groups, and we sensed on the
Friday night some disappointment both in our age and
approach. On Saturday morning a woman shared a dream
in which she was at a building a bit like a hotel (often a
metaphor for a dream group) where there were lots of
handicapped people in wheelchairs with blankets on
their knees. The dreamer went round caring for them as
they were being neglected. In the dream she was much
younger than in real life, about our age. Exploring the
dream with us, she was able to be in touch with her role in
life as a helper and with the younger part of herself that
had gone into caring for others as a vicarious way of
meeting her own needs. There was still something missing,
though. Joan and I wondered if there was a message for us
there too, especially as she had said that in the dream she
was about our age. We suggested this by saying that often
dreams dreamt on the Friday night of a weekend group
pick up some left-over feelings from the evening. Were
there any feelings left over about the way we had or had
not taken care of the group? She said yes, she had thought
we were a little offhand but had not been able to tell us.
Then we were able to go back to the dream and work in
much greater depth with the part of her that needed the
sort of caring she had given to others for most of her life.

There were many more examples from that weekend.
Without our being aware that on one level the dream
could relate to the group, I think we would have been
completely stuck. In each case we could explore the
dreamer's ambivalences, so that once they were expressed
openly the members were able to be more involved in the
group. Just like the conference dreams in Chapter 7,
coming to a dream group will usually produce dreams that
will relate to feelings about being there. One man had a

dream in which his father was telling him to do something he did not want to do. We asked him if there was any connection with the night before, and he acknowledged that he had had some resistance to carrying out some of my suggestions for dream recall. (There were, of course, other levels to the dream too.) Another man dreamt of missing a train (he had in fact arrived late for the group by train and there had been no one to meet him), and at the end of the dream he was being given food to eat which was supposed to be good for him. It consisted of a stew made with red and black trousers (Joan and I had been wearing these colours the night before). There seemed little doubt that he had ambivalent feelings about being at the group (being late in reality and in the dream) and that he was experiencing us as force-feeding him something not too pleasant. A final example to show how the unconscious can express the same theme is one in which a man dreamt that a team of young footballers were waiting for their clothes to be ironed. It was in some sort of a factory, where everything was very mechanical. In fact the dream group consisted of eleven people including myself and Joan (the football team). Once again there was a reference to age, and to our style of leading (mechanical). The dreamer also connected with not wanting to have his dirty washing done in public.

In all these cases the dreamers were amused at how they had chosen to express their feelings. The connections were made by the dreamers themselves once we had pointed out how dreams often pick up on unfinished business from the day before, and the result was that the group became very involved and enthusiastic as their negative feelings had been expressed and accounted for.

I have mentioned that clients often have dreams in the style of their therapist. There is a danger that therapists can ignore this or fit dreams into their favourite theory. If we are not aware of this, there could be a danger of members of our groups not only having social dreams because that is our focus, but also in our seeing the social aspect to the exclusion of other aspects. The dream sharing would soon become sterile, forcing what I have earlier called 'premature closure'.

The Telling of the Dream

As well as looking at possible messages in the dream, I pay attention to how the dream is told. This can tell me how much investment a person has in working on their dream. I would remind readers of the exercise at the end of Chapter 6, when I encouraged you to pay attention to what happens to you when a dream is told to you. I do this exercise very early on in a group, so that everyone is aware of the effect the content of the dream has on them and the manner in which it is related. Very often this is apparent from the opening statement – 'I don't think you'll make anything of this' (challenge), or 'Well I'd quite like to tell you this dream' (and quite like not to, maybe?), or 'I have this silly/boring dream' (fear of taking responsiblility). I have learnt that ignoring these cues can hinder progress as has happened when I have been trapped into working with a dream in which the dreamer had little investment. As well as the genuine desire to work on a dream, we all have a saboteur within us which operates just below the surface. In technical terms I am paying attention to process (the how of something) as opposed to content (the what of something). In this way I am not blinded to elaborate content told in a way that switches me and the group off.

I would like to make it clear that I am not making judgements about whether the dreamer *should* have a high investment in his dream, I am simply noticing what *is*. The beauty of working with process is that there is no goal – we do not have to find the meaning or get to the bottom of the dream – we simply notice what is happening. The telling can also give clues and messages about the dream content. For example, an apparently very sexual dream can produce no sexual feelings in either me or the group, whereas a dream that has no apparent sexual content can produce a sexual feeling in me and others depending on the way it is told. I notice these reactions and have learnt to trust them and encourage the group to do likewise. This is one of the big advantages of groups. It is highly unlikely that if many people have the same reaction that it has nothing to do with the dream or dreamer.

Why Now?

The question of why the person is having this dream now, can be extended into why is this person telling this dream now? It can be a personal need, a statement to the group, or an expression of the group's need made through the individual (like filling in an awkward silence). Just as the dream has many levels, so too has the telling, and during the life of a group each dream and its telling will perform different functions. It is here that we move away from the dream into group dynamics, so I would like to say that I hold all these questions (what is this person saying to the group, to me, how is this person telling the dream, what are my reactions, the group's reactions, why is the person choosing to share now) as part of a process which may or may not be relevant. Most of all it helps me decide which technique is most likely to be appropriate – whether to have the whole group involved directly, work at depth individually and have the group share, or maybe not work at all. Without such background information, the choosing of techniques is likely to be an arbitrary affair, not synchronizing with the life of the group.

TECHNIQUES

If This Were My Dream . . .

I have used this technique very successfully with all groups I have worked with. It involves the whole group, is easy to follow and provides a lot of safety for dreamer and group alike. For this reason I introduce it near the beginning of a group session. My thanks are due to Monte Ullman at whose workshop I learnt the technique. He has written about it in greater detail[1] and what follows is my version although I think I have by and large kept to his guidelines.

The technique involves asking for a recent, comparatively short dream from a group member – recent so that connections can be made with day residue and comparatively short so that the group does not get lost in detail. At this stage the group simply listens. I will have done the listening exercise suggested earlier but this time the group members are instructed to listen to it as if it were *their* dream – to identify with it and feel it as their own. If they want to write the dream down that is fine. I then have the dreamer repeat the dream again asking the group to listen in the way described above. The group than asks any questions that relate to the *content* (not the meaning or interpretation) of the dream, such as, 'Where were you standing when you saw the bus?' 'Were there any people in the street?' 'Do you know where the bus was going to?' As facilitator I make sure the process does not go on unduly or unnecessarily. I then ask the dreamer to tell the dream a final time.

The next stage is for members of the group to identify the feelings in the dream as if it were their own dream. I give them the structure 'In my dream I felt . . .' to ensure that they do not try and put the feelings onto the dreamer 'You must have felt. . . etc.' In this way feelings that may not have been mentioned directly in the dream are picked up. The point about everyone in the group 'owning' the dream is to treat everything as a projection not as a truth about dream or dreamer. If I own what I say as my own, then the dreamer is free to say, 'No, that does not belong to me', or 'Yes, that fits for me'. The feedback is not given as an absolute truth, but as a personal statement.

The next step is to go beyond the feelings and explore the dream as a whole. Again I offer the structure 'In my dream . . .' or slightly differently, 'If this were my dream . . .' The latter allows more scope for fantasy, but care must be taken that this structure is not used for interpretation. What often happens is that the group goes into a free-wheeling association – one person's comments sparking off another as different parts of the dream are worked on. I tell people to avoid looking at the dreamer for confirmation, as it is *their* dream for the moment. All the dreamer has to do is sit back and listen, although I encourage note-taking as it is impossible to remember everything that has been said.

The next stage is for the dreamer to relate what has resonated. He or she is under no obligation to say anything and particularly does not have to give feedback for the sake of the group. However, if some chord has been touched and the dreamer would like to share that, all well and good. Finally there is an attempt to relate the dream to what has been happening for the dreamer the day before – to trace the day residue. This may have happened spontaneously during the preceding stages, but may need some eliciting. Tracing the day residue helps the dreamer own the dream as his own because he is the only member of the group to have had that day residue. It also enables him to see the combination of day residue and any larger issues that may have been uncovered. (Did that conversation we had yesterday really remind me of how my teacher spoke to me ? etc.) It is important to leave the dreamer to make his own connections – not to foist them on him, however obvious they look.

I describe all five stages at the beginning so that members know what to expect and how to listen – the first three are relevant for them, the last two are for the dreamer. I will repeat them here. First, listen to the dream, and after the first or second listening ask questions that relate to the content of the dream. As you listen, imagine it is your own dream. Secondly, share with the group what feelings came up for you, using the 'In my dream' structure. Thirdly, feed back anything else that comes to mind, using the 'If it were my dream' structure. Then, the dreamer, who had up to now just been listening, reports anything that has been sparked off for them in the free association of the group. Finally the group helps the dreamer to connect the dream with the day residue (the term used for the events of the day that have triggered off the dream) so that the dream belongs to the dreamer once again.

Key Questions
The technique of Key Questions, (and indeed all the other techniques described in Chapter 5, 'Ways of Working On Your Own') can also be used in a group. It is used in exactly the same way as in individual work, but people in the group provide the questions. The skill in a group is to be able to ask meaningful questions, and for the facilitator to make sure the dreamer is not being overwhelmed. Generally

about eight to ten questions are enough. In an on-going
group the main focus using questions is what happens
between the group sessions, rather than in them. The
questions are given as homework to be meditated on and
answered and the first part of the next group is devoted to
hearing the answers.

Incubation

In a group, I extend the technique described on page 75 by
asking members to think of the problem with which they
want help from their dreams and then go through the
different questions alone (how do I feel about the problem,
what do I hope to gain from asking it? etc). I ask them to
write out the answers, and then share the work they have
just done with another member of the group – they can
reveal as much or as little as they want. The partner just
listens and helps to clarify any statements that seem
vague. In this way one other person is directly involved in
the incubation. I then tell the members to go through the
same steps as described in Chapter 5, i.e. reading over
what they have written just before going to sleep, being
clear about the final question and treating any dream that
they remember as being connected with the incubation,
however unlikely that may seem. The following week (if
an ongoing group) or day (if a weekend group) we share
dreams that have come from the incubation. Having one
person who has gone through the questions with the
sharer can be very supportive as well as helping to make
connections between the dream and the incubation
question.

Psychodrama

This a technique which by definition needs other people,
as the idea is for members of the group to play different
characters in the dream. It helps to bring the dream alive,
allowing group members to participate and play roles that
are relevant for them personally as well as for the dreamer.
The dreamer can play a part or watch their dream re-
enacted, noticing the similarities and differences to their
own dream, perhaps opening up possibilities that have

not occurred to them. As many people may be playing roles at the same time, this technique requires a director who is in charge, and makes sure that the purpose of using psychodrama is clearly kept in mind, so that the dreamer does not feel taken over or lost in the drama. In many ways close to the Gestalt technique with members instead of cushions becoming different parts of the dream, it has both advantages and disadvantages in comparison. In the description of the dream group at the end of the chapter, I use psychodrama at the end of the group and explain why I use it. On the whole I have used the Gestalt technique, which may be just a question of temperament and familiarity, and I advise readers who are interested in learning more to read some of the original works on psychodrama and dreams by the founder of the technique, Moreno.

Gestalt

This technique which involves becoming and dialoguing with a symbol can be done on one's own. However, having an outsider enables more cues to be picked up. In the following example a woman shared a dream that arose from doing a dream incubation the week before. Her question was, 'How is the Pill affecting me?' In her dream she is coming out of work and walking along Tottenham Court Road. By a pub called the Rising Sun she sees a small man with a nicotine moustache, stocky, with a huge beer barrel. The only other detail is that she knows there has been a rape – she's not sure whether she has been rapist, victim or observer.

I ask her to be the man and he turns out to be a composition of her brother and her lover. Nothing much emerges until one member suggests she become the beer gut. This intuition proves to be spot on, and one that would never have occurred to me. The beer gut becomes a male pregnancy which turns into anger that men don't have babies or stretch marks. Apparently the dreamer's mother is still very angry about her stretch marks from giving birth to twins, and the dreamer realizes how much she has absorbed without fully realizing her mother's feelings – especially feelings of guilt for what she and her twin have done to their mother. She makes connections with her incubation question, particularly where some of her ambivalences concerning pregnancy have come from, seeing the Pill as some kind of violation but up to now necessary. She also recognizes that more can be done with the dream, especially with the rape aspect.

It was being in a group that provided the breakthrough in the work. Not only with this particular Gestalt technique, but in many other instances, the group invariably provides extra resources, and the skill of the facilitator is in the ability to encourage people to try out their hunches and intuitions without losing the flow of the work.

Continuing the Dream – an Example

I often use this technique when someone has woken themselves up. In the following example the advantages of working with someone else can be seen. Sandy is someone I know well and she trusts the way I work, so that I do have permission to push. The dialogue shows some of the methods that are useful in working with dreams – particularly in making a vague statement specific. I add my own commentary so that readers will see why I make certain suggestions.

At the beginning of our on-going dream support group, Sandy asks if she can present a dream from three years ago. The group members nod, recognizing that this dream must be very important for her.

Robin: That's fine with me. [I wonder why she is choosing to present it now.] Is there some issue you are wanting to work on generally and are choosing to do via the dream? [I would only do this with a group who had been sharing regularly and are sophisticated enough to understand this idea.]

Sandy: (Pauses and smiles) Probably.

Robin: OK. [I feel she has taken some responsibility for the issue whatever it may be.] Let's hear the dream.

Sandy: I am in a two-storeyed house. There is a maniac murderer around. I am terrified. I realize I don't have to stay in the house – I can actually leave it. I go to hide in the dustbin outside. I lift the lid. There is a black plastic bag full of limbs. I run down toward the road where there is a car belonging to someone I know. As I get in the driver turns to face me and I see it is the maniac murderer I had run away from. I wake up.

Robin: I have an idea that the best way of working on the dream might be to continue it. How would you feel about that? [There are so many possibilities – the Gestalt technique of becoming the different parts being one of the obvious. I have a sense, however, that Sandy needs to face something and so continuing the dream seems a logical step. I make sure I check it out with her.]

Sandy: (Looks appealingly at Robin) Do I have to?

Robin: No, it's completely up to you.

Sandy: (Reluctantly) Very well. (Closes her eyes, pauses)

Robin: What is happening now?

Sandy: I've got out of the car and I'm running towards a house. (Pause)

Robin: And now? [I ask open ended questions, let her follow her own way.]

Sandy: I'm by the front door. (Shudders) I can sense him standing there waiting to get me.

Robin: Take a second to notice what is happening to you. Are you watching yourself or are you actually feeling yourself? [I sense she is actually fully in the situation from her breathing. I check this out. I find the best work is when someone is there *and* has some detachment. The question takes her out a little, but there is no risk that she will not be able to go back. The focus of the work is clear – the maniac murderer has appeared three times. There is no escape.]

Sandy:	I'm there. (She looks very frightened)
Robin:	You look frightened.
Sandy:	(Nods)

Robin:	Where can you feel the fear? [Puts her in touch with her body. Stops the terror from feeling overwhelming by making it specifically located.]
Sandy:	In my stomach.
Robin:	Can you give the fear a voice? What is it saying? [Encouraging her to be specific about the fear and put it out verbally.]
Sandy:	Please don't get me. Pleeeease.
Robin:	Is there anything familiar about that? [Encourages her to put the situation in perspective.]
Sandy:	Yes, it's a feeling I've often had. Can I stop now? (She asks this in a half-hearted way, using a little girl voice with appealing gestures.)
Robin:	Is this how you usually avoid tricky situations? [Referring to the way she asks. This is very confrontative but I guess that Sandy will be able to accept this. It also gives her some detachment by pointing out her defence mechanisms in a way she can accept.]
Sandy:	(Laughs) You bugger. (Goes silent)
Robin:	What's happening now?
Sandy:	I'm going in. He's waiting for me. I can't bear it.
Robin:	Can you see him?
Sandy:	(Screws up eyes) No I don't want to look.
Robin:	What don't you want to see? [A tricky question. Rather than encouraging her to look, which she might resist, I come at a curve. She doesn't answer directly but stops blocking.]
Sandy:	He's so big. He's enormous. He's towering over me.

Robin: What is he wearing? [Again asking for specifics.]

Sandy: Baggy trousers. I don't want to go on.

Robin: What happened then?

Sandy: I didn't want to see his face.

Robin: What didn't you want to see? [I guess she already knows somewhere. Again like asking the same question above I don't ask her 'why not' which would involve explanations.]

Sandy: (Long pause) His mouth.

Robin: What can you see? [I am implicitly suggesting to her that she looks.]

Sandy: It's all twisted and cruel [Talking in a little girl voice. I remember she said the man was huge. This gives me the cue for my next question.]

Robin: How tall are you? Where do you come up to on him?

Sandy: I am only little. I come up to his waist.

Robin: What are you wearing? [By asking her to be specific, I am trying to give her a feel of herself and focus less on the paralysing fear.]

Sandy: My blue dress that I wore when I was five. I used to be terrified of snakes then. This is the same kind of fear. No I don't want to go into the snakes. They were terrible. (Starts to go into them) I used to have nightmares about them.

Robin: (Teasingly to group) Notice how she is going off into the snakes. Scarey, but familiar territory. Anything to avoid his face.

Sandy: (Smiles in acknowledgement, and quickly becomes anxious.)

Robin: Tell me about his eyes. What colour are they? [A hunch on my part. Would have been safer to ask what was happening, but I guess that amount of hatred has to be, in part, located in the eyes. I start off with something specific like the colour.]

Sandy: I don't want to look. (Pause – shaking of head. I
          encourage her to look. Finally, she answers.) Brown,
          hazel brown. (Pauses).

Robin: What is happening now?

Sandy: It's my father. He's looking at me with such hatred.

Robin: What's his look saying? Can you put words to it?
          (Sandy cringes.) What's going on for you?

Sandy: I can't bear that amount of hatred.

Robin: I notice you are quite passive. He hates you and you
          stand there. How do you feel about him?

Sandy: (Voice a little stronger) I hate him.

Robin: Tell him [Speaking to someone directly is more
          powerful than speaking about them.]

Sandy: I hate you! (Voice tails). I don't think it will make
          any difference.

Robin: (Gently) I'm not asking you to change anything The
          little girl had to swallow her feelings. You don't
          have to do that now. Tell him how you feel.

Sandy: (Pauses. Suddenly cries) You big bully, (and again
          louder) you big bully. I'm only small. You don't
          have to use so much force. You're much stronger
          than me. It's not fair. You should know better. It's
          not right. (Smiles) I can look him in the eye now

Robin: Do you mind if we finish there? [More could be
          done, dialoguing with her father, but it is near the
          end of the group and the bulk has been done for
          this time anyway.]

I explain to the group (it is a training group) that I had no
idea of who the man was going to be, but knew that it was
important for her to confront him as every time she ran
away, he kept reappearing. I had not asked her to change
anything – just to stay in touch with what was happening,

and had encouraged her to notice how she avoided tricky situations. (This explanation also had the effect of debriefing Sandy by bringing the work back into the context of a training group.) I did not know where the words 'You big bully' had come from. In her account, Sandy said

> I remembered a time when I felt wrongly accused by him. I felt hopeless and started to withdraw. I was backing away, breaking contact with him, turning in on myself. Robin kept pushing me, telling me to keep looking at him – to call him by the name I'd used as a child. I didn't want to have any contact at all (also this was all quite new and startling – my hostility has always been expressed for my mother, not my father). I struggled to find my voice and not go for the familiarity of retreat. And then it came, 'You big bully'. I'd begun to work on my own violent emotions.

The following week Sandy came in smiling. She reported a great improvement in her sex life as she had begun to take the initiative rather than be passive. Over time she told me that she has learnt about making choices. She had been aware that she had had the choice when working with me to stop and had really felt how she had chosen to go on. She had also begun to be more openly irritable, and express more hostility to men. She reckoned that was beginning to happen anyway but the dreamwork had facilitated the process (she may have chosen to share her dream at that time because she was ready for change).

Throughout the work, Sandy managed to stay with her feelings. Her attempts to avoid them were mostly half-hearted and she had a genuine desire to confront the maniac/murderer. If she had really wanted to sabotage, she could have very easily turned me into a bully who was forcing her to do something she did not want to do. In this way the dream would have been replicated, with me in the role of bullying man. This replication of the dream is known as paralleling, and, although not a technique, is something to watch for in dream work.

Paralleling

Here are some more examples to illustrate this concept.

Dream Theme	*What happens in the Group*
The dreamer is at the wrong station. She does not want to be there at all and is stuck there with her luggage.	We get very stuck. I ask her if being at the group is like being at the station where she does not want to be. She agrees and as usually happens, this allows the work to progress.
A man dreams he is tricking a policeman into believing something.	Again all the promising avenues get blocked. I jokingly remarked that he might be tricking me at the moment into thinking he wanted to work. The group is relieved. Apparently this person often needs to hook outside male leader's attention. The dreamwork then proceeds at a very moving level.
A man dreams that he has to deal with an unexploded bomb.	We make no headway. The dreamer does not want to let his feelings out (unexploded bomb) and I do not push, as I want the work to come from him. The group gets increasingly agitated and turns on me in an explosive way. I point out how the dreamer is getting others to explode for him and he is still not expressing himself. The group see how the present and the dream tie in.

Sometimes the manner of telling will also parallel the dream. 'I dreamt that I was lecturing and no one took any notice of me' – told to the group in a way that did not hold anyone's attention (here both content and manner of telling are paralleled).

Working with this awareness brings the dream into the here and now. As such, I do not only work with the dream, but the interactions that are sparked off in the telling – the communications and sharing, as well as the deep personal work. The group recognizes this, and respects the communications that are shared either in or via the dream. Recognizing paralleling facilitates the dreamwork by taking into account the here and now. It does not however substitute for it.

DREAMS IN THE LIFE OF AN ON-GOING GROUP – A TRAINING WEEKEND

In describing some of the work done on this weekend, I will be explaining my choice of techniques and how they fitted into the life of the group. This particular group has been together for about one and a half years training in groupwork and different facilitator styles. The group has worked very closely together, and, as in any close group, there are still tensions and feelings that have not been cleared. In a month's time it will be going on a week's residential, the second in the life of the group. The group has been shaken by a serious suicide attempt by one of the members, Ingrid, who has recently returned to the group after recovering from the effects. Joan has been co-facilitator on this course, and I have been invited in for a special interest group on dreams. She has filled me in on some background information on the group. As this is a training group on groupwork skills, I decide to focus even more on the life of the group than usual – using dreams as reflections on the interpersonal as well as the intrapersonal. However, I also have a brief to demonstrate dreamwork techniques and hope I will be able to combine both.

There are fifteen members in the group. Most people are in the thirties/early forties age range, although there are two in their fifties and Anna is in her early sixties. The training weekend takes place in a new centre which several of the members have helped to set up, and from the beginning I sense that I am going into a group with a strong identity, even if at the moment it is a little fragmented. Over the weekend I work directly with eleven out of the fifteen members – Jude, Jacky, Anna, Phil, Kirti, John and Arthur on the Saturday, and Jan, Jude (again), Philip, Brenda and Ingrid on the Sunday.

The group begins on the Friday evening. I ask each person for three words that come to mind when they think of dreams. This very quickly tells me some of the main areas of interest. Not all the words are positive and people discuss their choice of words. I then ask them to go into pairs and describe their day as a dream, using symbols and metaphors for events in the day and putting them together in some kind of 'dream' sequençe. This exercise helps the group to understand the origin of metaphors in a dream, by connecting them with the day's events. In my description of my day, I use the metaphor of being stabbed, and realize how deeply I had been affected by something earlier which I had tried to put to the back of my mind. We finish with a dream shared in threes, with people noting their responses and the way they listen.

In the morning the first dream to be shared belongs to Jude. It is quite a long dream beginning with the words 'Joan is to enable the group to be reborn. I see her with lots of babies around her thighs'. It includes five members of the group and is rich in symbolism. We are using the 'if it were my dream' structure, but there is little energy in the group. Jude has told the dream in a rather flat voice, but the structure prevents me from saying anything about this or the group energy, and I am frustrated. However, I realize that in the dream which I have taken on as my own, I am doing a lot, but do not seem too involved in anything I am doing. Even when I expect to get angry when some men show me a large glossy book of erotic pictures, I don't. Something clicks – the energy in the group is paralleling the energy in 'my' dream and I say, 'If this were my dream, I would not feel particularly committed to anything'. Several of the group nod and this gives permission for the group to really own 'their' dream, and not to be too tied to Jude's dream. Jude is able to recognize that the quality in the dream corresponds with something in her life at the moment.

In the second dream, Jacky is staying in a dormitory with bunk beds, sharing with Anna and some others in a small room. Jacky comes into the room to find that Anna has moved her bed. She is furious. Anna says, 'But Jacky, there are rats'. A dialogue ensues in the dream with Jacky saying there couldn't be, and Anna assuring her that there were. In the search that follows Anna says, 'Don't worry, I've brought in the cats'. Using the 'if it were my dream' technique the group refers to the last residential when they had slept in dormitories and Anna had slept on her own in a tent. Anna had wanted some privacy, and Jacky connects this with the anger she had felt towards me when I suggested recording dreams in the middle of the night. She had felt I had intruded into her night's sleep. She also connects her resistance to recording a dream for the dream group with Anna's description of her resistance to bringing dreams to her analyst. Anna seems to have become a symbol for resistance in Jacky's dreams. More personal work was done on the cats/rats which was important for Jacky, but the communication aspect of dreams is also becoming apparent with the previous residential, Anna and myself all featuring.

Sure enough, after lunch Anna asks for some time. She has a violent headache. I ask her to become the headache and it turns into a very seductive man who sometimes appears in her dreams. A dialogue ensues between him and Anna which seems to be leading nowhere. I ask Anna how much energy is in her voice and she says 'thirty per cent'. I ask her where the rest is, and she says 'in her resistance'. I validate her resistance as it seems to be important, and suggest that she stays with it for the rest of the day. No one has suggested this to her before – they have either interpreted it or have tried to coax her out of it. Although the headache remains, she seems relieved that she has been given permission to do what most of her wants to do. It seems likely that she has come to represent resistance to the group and has got stuck with that label. I guess this from Jacky's dream and know that in groups people choose and get chosen for certain roles.

Phil decides too that he would like to share not so much a dream but four images – one of a well worn dark brown leather jacket; another of a bright lime green official form; an idea of confusion and separation which he finds disturbing until the phrase 'creative unity' comes up, which satisfies him; and finally the words of the song, 'Hey! good looking, what ya got cooking?' His associations to the well-worn jacket are of old age, the green form has something to do with green being the colour of the heart, the confusion and separation he sees as his feelings about the group at the moment, and the song is some sort of virility image. The group now takes over and says, 'That's exactly how we see you – we're always wondering what you have cooking. You hide your goodies; we'd like to see more of them'. Phil talks about a new relationship he is starting and the group encourages him to do a celebration dance while they sing the tune. The work has a lovely quality.

The next person to tell a dream is Kirti. In it, he is travelling from Bristol to Norwich by boat and then coming back by bus via London where he is having trouble buying tickets. I know a little about him from Joan and guess that he is a very experienced group member. For people like that (and I include myself here) it is very often the work done between the groups that is important. We have learnt a way of being in groups – we have, as it were, learnt the ropes. So I suggest the technique of Key Questions which he can take away and answer between Saturday and Sunday. The group suggest numerous questions and Kirti writes them down. The energy level in the group is dropping – is this to do with feelings about Kirti, his dream, the way of working or just because it is mid-afternoon?

At this point John decides to share. I immediately wonder why now. In his dream he is in a house, looking for a room, searching right through the house. The theme of searching seems important rather than the actual room. I wonder if the dream is not going to be paralleled in the group and he might not find what he is looking for here too, as the energy is so low. I decide to combine the dream theme, the intuition about the time of sharing, the low group energy and what little I know about John, into a structure. I ask him if he knows what he is looking for in the group. He says acceptance. I suggest that he might want different things from each member of the group which the blanket term 'acceptance' does not make clear, and he agrees. I then ask him to go and tell each member of the group what he would like to hear from them, for example, 'Jacky, I would like you to say that you like me' or 'Kirti, I would like you to say you admire the way I built my house'. The members then have the choice of whether they do it or not. I trust their honesty; that they will only say something if they want to. In this way, John is to take full responsibility for the positive feedback rather than sit back and wait for it just asking for acceptance; and the group can become very involved – choosing whether to speak or not. The group does become involved: the search in the dream has become the search in the group.

Finally, with a few minutes to go Arthur shares two dreams. In the first he is on a boat in the North Sea in the First World War. Something has happened that has made him think it is for real. He is appalled at the simple patriotism and naivity of his fellow soldiers and feels sick. In the second dream he is also on board ship but it is during the Second World War. He is engaged in an operation which involves him reacting immediately – firing at Japanese kamikaze pilots. The situation is to kill or be killed. There is not time to work with the dreams, but I am glad he has shared them. I sense the importance of the dreams for him and that he might be declaring a part of himself the group doesn't usually see. His involvement in the dreams contrasts with his apparent withdrawal during the day, and the group is moved simply by the sharing.

Jan starts the next day with a dream which involves John who worked on the theme of searching the previous day. In the dream John is lying in a wooden coffin with a glass top in the group room and everyone is gazing at him reverently. The scene changes to inside a chapel and someone, perhaps Jacky, is going to read something. Some white hens strut into the church and feathers float into the air. Someone (Jacky?) shoos them out. Suddenly the coffin goes back on rollers and this brings John to life.

At this point Jude sits up and says, 'I had a dream about John too'. She seems to be cutting across Jan and I remember that in Jude's dream of yesterday she was competing with Jan at the end. It does not seem relevant to mention this and I let them decide what to do. Jan nearly lets Jude continue, but then the group agree to let Jan finish.

Jan says how much she has been affected by the work with John. She says she does not know how to make contact with him. I guess that John is part of her, but do not want to embarrass her by saying this while she is talking to John. Arthur suddenly has a 'Eureka' experience and remembers that in the first year Jan had felt that Jacky had been 'pecking' at her. Jan then connects the white feathers with cowardice and realizes that she has killed off part of herself in the group – no wonder she finds John difficult and has dreamt about him. She takes back her projection and really feels the John part of her. The coffin has been rolled back and she has become alive. She has seen how a dream not only gives information about relationships with other people, but that it can also show how these people symbolize parts of ourselves. Jan is amazed. In a second the earlier incidents with Jacky, her feelings about John and her relationships with the group have been crystalized.

We return to Jude. In her dream she is hitting John and her boyfriend Kirti with a plank of wood. I know from Joan that Jude and Kirti have not worked on their relationship in the group, and notice Jude holding back. She clears it with Kirti that she can refer to the night before when they had a row. I ask her if she wants to act the dream out and give her a tennis racket for the plank of wood and a cushion for Kirti and John and she hits them both. The words 'give me some space' come up, and she realizes that these are words she wanted to say to her father. I am uneasy about going into such regressive material in this case, partly because it seems familiar ground. Jude seems 'stuck' too, and we agree to leave it there. Afterwards Jude tells me that the main value of the work was in being able to bring her relationship with Kirti more openly into the group via the dream.

Philip then shares a dream which is long and complicated and involves tricking policemen and which I have referred to earlier when talking about paralleling (page 136). Although a rich dream, we are stuck until the group realizes that the dream is being re-enacted. This frees everyone, including Philip, and he asks if we can do the 'if it were my dream' technique. We do and the whole group is involved, particularly the men, who identify with him.

In the afternoon Brenda shares a dream in which she catches a train from Waterloo, gets out at the wrong station, and is unable to catch one to the right station. Again the group realizes that this is a metaphor and statement of her feelings about being at the group. Suddenly Ingrid gets up and says, 'I'm the train' and careers round the room followed by three or four others. Someone becomes Waterloo station and someone else East Putney – the wrong station. The train runs backwards and forwards between each station with Ingrid making choo choo noises. Brenda watches and in the end joins in as Ingrid will not stop until she does. Behind the fooling around, Ingrid is showing a 'caring' attitude – saying 'I don't want this to be the wrong place for you. I want you here'.

Ingrid and the rest of the group are now full of energy, and Ingrid decides to share a dream which she has been debating whether to share all weekend. In the dream her ex-husband is helping her move into an attic flat. She goes downstairs and finds a baby sitting on the floor. She is overcome with joy in finding her and feels terrible sorrow at having had to abandon her. She goes for a ride in the country with the baby on a large tricycle and stops at a shed. The baby is sitting on the floor. A cat comes in and plays with the baby, then suddenly and viciously attacks it.

Ingrid dreamt this three weeks previously, but I can feel how much it relates to the present in her decision to tell it. I think she is saying, 'I am ready to face something'. In view of what has happened with her suicide attempt, the sharing is important not only for her but for the group also. I want to involve them as much as possible. As Ingrid tells the dream, my analytic mind equates the baby in the dream with Ingrid as a baby; the cat with Ingrid's mother who might have been friendly, but who had then attacked Ingrid in a treacherous manner; and finally the cat with

Ingrid as she is now. I guess she has swallowed her mother's feelings (introjected them) and now attacks herself (suicide attempt) in a treacherous way (the attempt comes out of the blue). This is speculation, but is the reason why I asked Ingrid to become the cat. I wanted her to get in touch with that part of herself.

Ingrid says she does not want to be the cat – it is too scary. I ask the group if they are willing to be cats with her and four or five cats appear. What she has done for Brenda is being done for her. This helps Ingrid ease her way into the role. I then ask her to choose someone to be the baby. She chooses Carole. Ingrid (cat) approaches the baby and suddenly attacks her. I ask her to describe her feelings and she says, 'I felt I had to attack the baby to show her she couldn't attack me'. I ask her to do it again in slow motion and to give a running commentary. As she attacks she says, 'Silly baby. Can't you see that I have my tail up? It looks as if I am friendly but just watch my tail'. I ask her to do it again. What has seemed like a sudden attack does in fact have a build-up. This will be relevant for the sudden attack on herself.

I then ask her to change places. Carole becomes the cat and Ingrid the baby. She feels bewildered at the cat's behaviour and connects with the inconsistency of her mother, who was sometimes pleased with her even when she was bad, and was often hostile when she was good. Ingrid identifies with her, knowing how quickly she can switch moods, like her mother. Her switches from being apparently fine to being suicidal are beginning to make sense to her and to the group as her behaviour has left them very uneasy. The cat/mother/Ingrid is a powerful force. I suggest she go through this scene again in slow motion to understand more aspects of the cat and to find out more about what the cat/mother/Ingrid wanted to do to baby Ingrid. The work has been totally absorbing and important for everyone in helping to come to terms with Ingrid's suicide attempt.

We end soon after. I am pleased with the way members have connected dreams to the life of the group. I know that people have realized that dreams shared in this way belong to the group as much as to the individual. I sense the group has come through a very splintered phase and that only time will tell whether it was a temporary high or will be of lasting benefit. In working interpersonally, I am calling on my skills as a groupworker as well as dream-worker. For me they have always gone together. In the following chapter on starting a peer group, I will be reiterating some of the group dynamics. Sometimes people interested in dreams attempt to bypass this aspect. My experience is that even though dreams are individual, sharing is communal and therefore these dynamics are at least as important as in any other group.

After the group has finished its two years together, Joan receives a postcard from Jacky (as does every other member of the group). Written on it is a dream . . . 'It is the last meeting of our group. Joan and Peter (the other facilitator) are in the kitchen cooking Sunday lunch for us. It is going to be the full works. I can smell the roast beef, Yorkshire pudding, etc. In the main room I am returning pieces of clothing I have borrowed from other group members over the last two years. Similarly I am getting clothes of my own returned. Someone (it has to be Philip) reminds me to check in the cupboard. I do and there is a whole rail full of clothes there. I pack everything in a suitcase ready to go . . . With many thanks for the loans and the nourishment, Love Jacky, P.S. If this were my dream . . . RSVP'.

10.

STARTING YOUR OWN GROUP

'As each man tells his tale, there must be another there to listen. But the other need not be a guru. He need only rise to the needs of the moment.'

Sheldon Kopp[1]

Although I had been interested in my dreams for over ten years, it was not until I set up a dream group with some of my friends that what had been merely a strong personal interest developed into a major focus of my professional work. It was through this peer group which lasted for about two years that I came to appreciate fully the value of sharing dreams, the bonds that form amongst the sharers and my skill in working with other's dreams. It remains one of the best groups I have ever been part of, both because of the excitement and risk involved in setting it up, and the depth of sharing that occurs when a dream group is running well.

As long ago as 1973 I had written to Ann Faraday after the publication of her book *The Dream Game* to ask if she knew of any dream groups. Her husband replied, saying he did not know of any, but asking why didn't I start my own, as this is how they had started. This was in the days when the encounter movement had not really taken off in England, and I had no experience of group work. However, the Gestalt method of becoming part of the dream seemed quite straightforward and a friend and I tried it with each other quite successfully. The years went by and I gradually began to train in groupwork methods, particularly psycho-drama, so that when our peer group started I was quite experienced both as a member and a leader of groups. This certainly helped, and in fact all our members were similarly involved with groups. However, although there is no substitute for group experience I think anyone who has a real interest in dreams can set up a peer dream group, if, strict guidelines are kept to, at first. Establishing one for clients in a day centre or therapeutic community requires additional skills, but certainly setting up a group of committed dream sharers, all willing to take some responsibility for the group, is not a difficult target to achieve. I have included a list of resources at the back of the book. These include people who have worked extensively with dreams and may (as I have done for some groups just beginning) be willing to give advice on setting up a group. A copy of *In Our Own Hands*[2] by Sheila Ernst and Lucy Goodison is about the best book resource that is readily available.

Joining or Starting a Group

If you want to join a peer group, then you can contact any of the resources mentioned at the back of the book. They may know of a group already running. The disadvantage of joining an already-formed group is that the group will have its own way of working. These groups are also often closed to outsiders as a group will quickly develop trust, and an outsider will not be able to share easily at the same level. However people do drop out, and this can be a good way of starting. Check out how it feels to be part of such a group. Will you be able to entrust an important part of yourself to these people? How welcome and receptive are they? Do they have a particular philosophy and way of looking at dreams or are they open to different ideas? Check yourself too. What are your expectations and how great is your commitment and motivation?

If you want to start your own group, mention the idea to friends and if there is enough response, arrange a meeting. I know of people who have had lunch-time groups at work/college. Even if for some reason you cannot get together a group who know each other, I would not recommend advertising. I prefer being in a peer group with either friends or people I know in some way. In this way sharing can enrich our friendship. But this is just my preference. If for any reason you cannot join or start a peer group, you could begin by going to a group led by a professional facilitator, and pick up ideas (and maybe dreamers). If you have followed the steps in this book, you may well have started sharing with a friend or a member of your family. Not only will you have some experience of techniques, but you may well have the 'core' of a group. I have found a good number to be between five and seven. There needs to be enough people to form a group so that if someone drops out, the group will have enough of an identity to continue. On the other hand there needs to be enough time for as many people to share as want to, so I would recommend eight as an absolute maximum.

First Meeting

The following guidelines are ones I drew up for an article in *Self and Society*, and have been the basis for many peer groups. To start with, I think it is important to have someone who is responsible for managing the practicalities at the first meeting. This is the time for people to be as clear as possible about what they want from a group and what kind of a group they are expecting. There are, as we have seen, many different ways to share dreams – each going into different depths. Perhaps the single most important fact in the group is the degree of commitment. If there is goodwill and high interest, many of the practicalities will fall into place.

Here, then, are some guidelines for the first meeting. There will be points that may not be relevant for you, and

others you may wish to include. People can come to this
meeting either with a commitment to meet for a certain
length of time (say six evenings), or just come to the first
meeting and then decide about their commitment. Much
will depend on how well people know each other beforehand and if they have had a chance to discuss it. Either
way, once it has been agreed the group is viable, it is a good
idea to review the group after a certain number of
sessions. In this way the group does not drift aimlessly,
and there is an opportunity to process what is happening
without waiting for an outside event, like someone leaving
or wanting to join, to force the group to question itself, its
norms and ways of working.

1. Ask people to share their reasons for coming, previous
   experiences of working with dreams and being in a
   group, skills they have to offer, expectations and special
   interests.

2. Arrange a certain number of meetings.

3. Agree a venue. If possible and acceptable to all, it is a
   good idea to have one place as it builds up associations.

4. Decide upon frequency and duration of the group.
   Groups vary – weekly or fortnightly seems best. A good
   duration for a weekly group is 1½-2 hours; maybe
   slightly longer if fortnightly. Our group enjoyed meeting
   in the early morning when we didn't have the daytime
   clutter to wade through and so had a good focus on
   dreams, but obviously that would be difficult for many.
   I would like to give a word of warning about not having a
   regular time, but merely resorting to diaries at the end
   of each meeting in order to arrange the next one. This
   can waste a lot of energy and lead to resentment when
   someone proves to be inflexible. It is better to fix a
   regular time from the start. I know of two groups which
   started after a lecture on dreams. One lasted for over a
   year and a half, the other two months. A member of the
   latter group said how difficult they found it to meet
   regularly, and this may have been the difference between

the two groups, as the other agreed upon a regular time at the beginning.

5. Be clear about boundaries, i.e., starting and finishing on time. Persistant late starting can be a source of resentment, and prompt finishing encourages people to take responsibility for their own work and sharing. It avoids what we used to call in the therapeutic community where I worked 'Doorknob therapy' where the client saves what he wants to say until the group are about to leave and keeps everyone hanging on way past time.

6. Decide on a policy about notetaking. Although we never kept notes, I have met groups who have, and I think there is something to be gained from it. Notes provide an opportunity to see how the group progresses, and enable you to watch and record group images. Very often a symbol in one person's dream will reappear in someone else's. If notes are not kept at the time because they would be thought distracting, an agreement could be made about writing up shared dreams after the meeting.

7. Confidentiality is essential. A feeling of safety is of great importance in being able to share freely, and confidentiality contributes greatly to this. Each group needs to find its own guidelines, but most allow some reference to the group without going into personal details.

Remembering and Recording
Once these issues have been talked about and an agreement to meet has been reached, the group can begin with a dream if there is time, or leave it until the following week. In groups where I have been a designated leader I ask people to keep a dream diary for the length of the course and spend a few minutes talking about them (see Chapter 4). If appropriate I tell people that everyone dreams, give common causes for forgetting, and include a suggestion that they either dialogue or write a letter to their dreams if they are having any difficulties in remembering them. If someone is a good recaller but forgets their dreams on

coming to the group, it may be worth asking them if there is anything in the group that is inhibiting them. I only do this if it was bothering me or them and I usually wait or give some of the above suggestions like having a dialogue with their dreams.

Ritual

I vary on how much I like this, sometimes finding it precious, sometimes enjoying it thoroughly. Each group has its own ways of starting and finishing. Some begin with a meditation, some with a checking-in routine which enables people to say what is going on for them, in order to leave the day behind. A group leader friend of mine has a special dream pouch which is taken by anyone who wants to share a dream. It is filled with specially chosen objects that have significance to the group – stones, shells, bits of driftwood. She lights a candle at the beginning of the dream sharing and extinguishes it at the end. Her rituals have the effect of deepening the group's state of receptivity and also distinguish the sharing from any business before and after the group meeting.

Choosing How to Work

How a dream is shared and worked with will depend on the skills of the group, its focus and above all the wishes of the sharer. The group may have to decide whether everyone should share a dream each week or whether they should work with each dream for as long as feels appropriate. A balance between these two extremes can be reached if those who would like to share a dream say so at the beginning of the group, so time can be allocated to allow for this.

I mentioned above that how a dream is worked with depends, in part at least, on the wishes of the dreamer. When the group has many techniques at its disposal, I ask the dreamer to choose one of them. In a leaderless group, it is a good idea for the sharer to choose someone to be primary facilitator (rather like having a chairperson) who can either work intensively with the sharer, or co-ordinate the input of the group. The person chosen should be able to say no for whatever reason, as any ambivalence or reluctance will probably be picked up. Often it is enough just to share the ambivalence (e.g. I'm not feeling too confident today) in order to be clear enough to act as the primary facilitator. Having one primary facilitator should not rule out contributions from other members. After the group has been together, it usually finds the balance, with members tuning into the dream and the dreamer, and then contributions blend together rather than pull in different directions.

The balance between having someone as main facilitator, using the resources of the whole group and leaving the dreamer in charge of the sharing is, I have always found, best achieved in the group by using the 'If this were my dream' approach described earlier. Here the role of the facilitator is to ensure that the guidelines are followed and the dreamer is free to take or leave what she wants.I use this technique at the beginning of the groups I lead as it is so good at warming up the whole group. Later, I move on to other techniques.

Watching the Process

A useful reminder is to watch out for *how* a dream is shared. Many time I have seen exploration of dreams fizzle out because of the way a dream is presented or how the dreamer responds after presenting a dream. A person will sometimes act out their ambivalence about sharing their dream by presenting it in a way that gives the group little scope to move, either by having low energy, or saying that nothing feels right, or leading the group astray by bringing in a host of red herrings. Here the confidence of the group is needed so that people can share their reactions, such as 'I feel really stuck' or 'I noticed I was losing attention'. (The exercise described at the end of Chapter 6 is useful here as it heightens awareness of one's own reactions and avoids blaming other people.) Trusting one's own reactions can give important clues to either the dream or the sharing. We have already seen this under the section on paralleling, whereby the presentation of a dream can give clues either about how the dreamer felt *in* the dream, how he feels *about* the dream or how he feels about *sharing* it. For example, if you notice yourself switching off, one possible reason is that the dreamer does not want to get to the bottom of the dream or share personal details. The skill of trusting your own reactions is one of the most important in a dream group, as are the skills of learning if, when and how to share these reactions. Some are not easy to share – in particular there are taboos about sharing boredom, sexual feelings and frustration. And in all cases, it is only relevant to share them if they come from hearing the dream, and are not left over from some other occasion.

Here are some examples. A man says he thinks he wants to share a dream and spends a while fishing around in his notebook. He finally reads out his dream, cannot easily read his own handwriting and stops and starts. I notice that I and others in the group have difficulty following him. We start working on the dream by asking for associations and quickly get stuck. I share my impressions about the way he told his dream and he admits to not having much interest in it himself. The content of the dream is about his inability to make a decision, and I point out that he cannot commit himself in the dream and that this seems to be happening in the group too. This grabs his attention, and the work with the dream starts afresh with new commitment. In another session of the same group, someone else shares a dream and there is some nervous giggling which seems totally out of keeping with the dream. The group has learnt to trust these clues and I ask what is going on. It turns out that there were many sexual feelings about the dream. The dreamer was unaware of the sexual aspect of his dream in which he brought a bottle of wine to share with his neighbour. The group had picked up how he naïvely suppressed his sexual feelings for this woman. Obviously this way of working requires a lot of trust so that the group does not foist its values onto the dreamer and the dreamer can trust the integrity of the feedback.

This brings me onto a very important point – the danger of making assumptions about people. Especially in groups where people have begun to know each other well, there is a temptation to fit the images of the dream to what is known about the dreamer (such as saying with a knowing look 'That bear that came towards you – you have been having a difficult time with your husband haven't you?) These semi-interpretations are sometimes very difficult to avoid or refute, as the connections are very plausible and based not on theory but on knowing people well. This process can to some extent be avoided by listening to the dream itself, rather than trying to connect it to a person's life too prematurely; and by using techniques like 'If it were my dream', 'Following the dream ego' and Key Questions, which are all mainly concerned with the dream.

Holding Back

From time to time a group may come to a standstill, or you as an individual may notice yourself or someone else holding back. If this is so, it can be useful to share your feelings about the group, yourself or the other person. You may be surprised to find out that your feelings are echoed by others who have not been able to share them, for fear of being out on a limb. Every group gets stuck once in a while, and this is a point where people often leave unless there are the skills and goodwill to work through the difficult patch. This is where it is very useful to have clear contracts and boundaries to refer to. Usually any reservations are better for being aired, as otherwise they tend to surface in another way. Sometimes the group as a whole may feel stale, or in need of new skills, and it could be useful to invite in an outside facilitator for one or two sessions. There are groups where complications do not seem to arise, but it is as well to be aware that they might, and not feel that your group is a failure if they do.

Leadership

This is sometimes a taboo subject in peer groups. It *may* be an issue if one person seems to be doing most of the facilitating or it is possible that people will hold back on their skills for fear of being seen to take over. As I suggested earlier, the dreamer could decide on the technique and the person they would like to facilitate, and in this way different people would be facilitating at different times.

Group Dynamics

I have spent some time looking at group issues, rather than just focusing on dreams themselves, because I believe the depth of sharing depends as much on how well the group is functioning as on skills in working with dreams. Without trust and a feeling of safety the group will soon stagnate no matter how experienced it is. Do not expect always to finish the dreamwork in the group. I say this because most of us have a strong need to have all the ends sewn up and this is not possible, or even desirable. Some of the best work can be done between meetings when the dreamer has a spontaneous insight, or has a dream which sheds light on a previous one. What is important is that individuals feel comfortable about not knowing the outcome of the dreamwork. In fact, dream sharing is operating on many levels anyway, and not all can be covered at once. I do strongly recommend getting to know some of the issues that affect groups (e.g., leadership, inclusion/exclusion, pairing between members)[3] as the common task of sharing dreams does not make the group immune from group dynamics. The inexperienced group, and even the experienced one, sometimes does not realize this, and just focuses on the individual and his or her dream. The dream itself may be private and personal, but once shared it is brought into the realm of the social.

My Own Experience

The peer group that I started five years ago was one of the most formative experiences in my work with dreams. We were all friends but had never been in a peer group together. Although we were close, working with our dreams allowed us space to be intuitive and receptive in a way that was normally reserved only for clients. We came to know each other in a different way through the imagery in our dreams. I would like to add that one of our original group of five left in a way that I found quite distressing, and the group stopped when one of the remaining four left London. I say this because although it was a good group, I do not want to pretend that we were without difficulties. However, the two years I spent with that group and hearing of other peer groups has convinced me that it is possible for anyone with sufficient interest and commitment to set up their own dream group.

EPILOGUE

OUTSIDE THE GATES OF EDEN

'At dawn my lover comes and tells me of her dreams
With no attempt to shovel that glimpse into the ditch of what
   each one means
At times I think there are no words but these to tell what's true
And there are no truths outside the Gates of Eden'
                              Bob Dylan 'The Gates of Eden'

This book has been my story of working with dreams. Behind the guidelines and examples, it stands as a statement of my own experience, told as I see it now. Like listening to a dream, you will have heard not only what I have said, but how I have said it; you may have been aware of levels that I have missed. If this book were your dream . . .

All attempts to influence people's ideas come, I believe, from some deep self-doubt within. I have, in my own way, tried to play down this 'converter' side of myself. Of course, I say, the world can exist without dream-sharing. However I know that I would be delighted to see a headline: 'Mankind saved by dream sharing. President uses hotline to share dreams'. And I struggle with the part of me that wants to influence on a gigantic scale, and the part of me that is happy to let people draw their own conclusions.

All books are, I believe, the story of oneself. Short of absolute truths which may exist in Eden, we are all here making our partial subjective statements to the world. And so I have written about my personal view of dreams. In this view it is the sharing that is most important for me. I have also come to recognize that through this sharing I am engaging with others in communicating in the 'Forgotten Language'. As I have shown, this communication has many practical aspects. But ultimately the value could still be something more than I imagine.

> When God lived, and man belonged, psychology was no more than a minor branch of the art of storytelling and mythmaking. Today, each man must work at telling his own story if he is to be able to reclaim his personal identity . . . Everything depends on the telling. The principle of explanation consists of getting the story told – somehow, anyhow – in order to discover how it begins. The basic presumption is that the telling of the tale will itself yield good counsel.[1]

So I have told my tale. By telling others, I remember to listen myself, for we teach what we most need to learn. And, if as a therapist, I should think that I understand the meaning of a dream, I remind myself that I am merely playing my own part in people telling their myths and stories to me and to each other.

APPENDIX 1

SUMMARY OF TECHNIQUES

Attitudes to dreams

1. Draw a circle with the word dreams written in the middle and spokes coming from the centre. Write out any word that comes to mind, returning to the word in the middle for each new association (described on pages 13-14).

2. In a group: go round the circle asking each person to say three words that come to mind when they think of dreams. This quickly gauges group interests (page 138).

Remembering and recording

1. For eliciting hidden resistance, finish the sentence: I don't want to remember my dreams because . . . (page 54).

2. Talk to dreams by putting them on a cushion, saying something then switching places and replying. This Gestalt technique is useful for finding out about attitudes which may be behind forgetting, but also for general attitudes to dreams (page 58).

3. Write up the day's events before going to sleep. The discipline can act as an aid to recall of dreams and connects them to events of previous day (page 59).

4. As above, but write up the day as if it were a dream. Connects the day with the language of dreams (page 138).

5. Notice your mood before going to sleep as this affects dreams (page 55).

6. Use suggestion before going to sleep, e.g. 'tonight I will remember my dreams'. Or visualize yourself waking up and recording a dream (page 55).

7. Record a dream as quickly as possible after waking as memory of most dreams fades quickly. Especially true of dreams from the middle of the night (page 59).

8. Give the dream a title.

Techniques That Can be Used by Yourself

1. Theme approach. Using only the content of the dream, write out short sentences beginning with 'someone (or something) is . . . ' e.g. someone is being chased; someone is trying to find someone. This quickly elicits the essence of a dream by ignoring the detail. Do any of the themes connect with everyday life? (page 62).

2. Following the dream ego. What is the dreamer doing in the dream? Focuses on actions rather than symbols (page 63).

3. Notice whether you are active or passive in the dream. Not simply in the doing/not doing sense, but notice if you are avoiding rather than meeting situations, and whether your actions are set in motion by someone or something else (page 64).

4. Ask yourself how you are feeling in the dream. Is the feeling quality familiar either with other dreams or everyday life? (page 64).

5. Sticking to the content of the dream, ask questions

which expand the dream. For example, in a dream where the dreamer is walking down a street ask if there are any people around. Where is the dreamer walking to? Is it night or day? How does this connect with daily life? (page 66).

6. Rewrite the dream from the point of view of one of the characters. This stays with dream content, but views it from a different angle (page 71).

7. Gestalt. Involves becoming one or more symbols of the dream and dialoguing with them. Enables parts of the dream to be experienced very fully, but often does not stay with dream as a whole (pages 68-71).

8. Free association. Asking oneself what comes to mind when thinking of a certain symbol, trying to catch first thoughts however irrational and unconnected they might seem (page 71).

9. Continuing the dream. Can be done in writing or by lying down and relaxing and letting the images appear – a waking dream. Offers opportunity to consciously integrate unfinished dreams (page 72).

10. Incubation. Asking dreams for help with a problem. Involves asking and answering questions about the problem and reading the answers over before going to sleep. Questions I have found useful are: What do I hope to gain from resolving the issue? What hidden benefits do I get from having the problem? How long have I had it? Consciously working on the problem frees the unconscious to prevent its view (page 75).

11. Expressing the dream through art, poetry, dance. Can lead to a deeper understanding of the dream, but can also be done for its own sake (page 75).

Telling Dreams

1. Tell someone a dream. Have them simply listen. Then swop. Act of telling a dream to a receptive audience can be beneficial (page 85).

2. As above, but ask the other person to tell your dream back to you. Absolute accuracy in details is not so important as hearing how your dream sounds. Swop roles (page 85).

3. Have someone tell you a dream and notice your responses, e.g. 'I felt . . .', or 'when you said . . .' 'I imagined . . .' Notice if your response wants to tell the other person what their dream means. Just giving your feelings, physical sensations and fantasies can throw light on the dream for the other person as well as tell you how you listen. Swop roles (pages 89-90).

For Groups
All individual techniques can be adapted for a group. However, two techniques that are particularly appropriate for a group are
1. 'If it were my dream . . .' A person tells a dream. Listeners take on the dream as their own, first clarifying details in the dream, then reporting back their feelings in 'their' dream and then any images and associations. All comments are treated as projections – to do with the listeners and not the dreamer. The dreamer takes what is relevant. In the final stage the dreamer is asked to make connections with events of the previous day (day residue) for the dream trigger (pages 125-27).

2. Psychodrama. Members of the group become the symbols or people in the dream. The dreamer can watch the dream re-enacted or take part. There is a need for a director to be clear about the focus of the work – how much the work is for the group and how much for the individual (page 128).

Group Dynamics
1. See either the content of the dream or the telling of it as a message to the group. Focuses very much on the interpersonal aspect of dream sharing so I only use it explicitly if it seems relevant for the dreamwork (pages 121-23).

2. Related to this – how is the dreamer telling the dream? Is this of any relevance to the dream, feelings about the dream (e.g. fear of revealing too much), or feelings about the group (page 124).

3. Why now? This question can throw light on what a person wants from the telling and what investment they have in the exploration of their dream (page 125).

4. From all of the above, is the dream being re-enacted in the group? This process of paralleling connects the dream with the telling (page 136).

As often as not these questions only occur to me when I or the dreamer seem stuck. Otherwise I take the dream and its telling more at face value. However, if dream sharing is to be done as consciously as possible, it is useful to have some knowledge of the above at your disposal. The aim is to always facilitate the dreamwork, not to analyse the dreamer. As such the timing and phrasing are important so that the feedback can be accepted as part of the work.

APPENDIX 2

RESOURCES

Bookshops

Changes   242 Belsize Park Road, London NW6 (01-328-5161). Recommended, as they do a very efficient mail order service and have a large selection of dream books.

Compendium   234 Camden High Street, London NW1. Stock a wide range of books in the humanistic psychology field.

Dillons   1 Malet Street, London WC1. Have a special section on dream books as well as a wide selection of psychology books.

Books

The Dream Game, Ann Faraday (Harper Row, 1976).

Dream Power, Ann Faraday (Berkeley, 1972).
   One of the best introductions to dreams.

Dream Work, Jeremy Taylor (Paulist Press, 1983).

A good chapter on groups and very clear on the archetypal levels of dreams, shadow and projection.

Dreaming and Waking, Corriere, Karle, Woldenberg and Hart (Peace Press, 1980).
The authors deal with the community aspect of dream sharing particularly well.

The Dreamwork Manual, Strephon Kaplan Williams (The Aquarian Press, 1984).
An excellent and comprehensive exposition of dreamwork techniques.

Experiment in Depth, P. W. Martin (Routledge Keegan Paul, 1955).
A pioneering book in exploring the unconcious in small groups.

The Forgotten Language, Erich Fromm (Grove Press, 1951).
Particularly good for the symbolic language in myths, legends and fairy stories as well as dreams.

In Our Own Hands, Sheila Ernst and Lucy Goodison (Women's Press, 1981).
Useful guidelines for setting up a peer group of any sort as well as a clear exposition of many of the humanistic psychology techniques.

The Instant Dream Book, Tony Crisp (Spearman, 1984).
Very readable with excellent examples of the value of working with dreams.

Introductory Lectures in Psychoanalysis, Sigmund Freud (Pelican, 1973).
A very clear and understandable account of many of Freud's ideas on dreams.

The Meaning of Dreams and Dreaming, Maria Mahoney (Citadel Press, 1972).
One of the best introductions to Jung's work on dreams.

Welcome to the Magic Theater, Dick McLeester (Food For Thought Publications, P.O. Box 331, Amherst, Mass 01002, USA).

A very full resource directory of different books, periodicals and articles on dreams.

Working with Dreams, Monte Ullman (Hutchinson, 1983). Extensive use of 'if it were my dream' technique and very clear on the benefits of dream sharing in a group.

Journals/Periodicals
On Dreams

Coat of Many Colours. A special edition of the bulletin available from Jeremy Taylor, 10 Pleasant Lane, C.A 94901, USA who has also published an interesting booklet on the boat community of Sausalito mentioned in Chapter 6.

Dream Network Bulletin. As well as publishing short articles on dreams, the bulletin has a useful list of resources and contacts of people working in the field of dreams, virtually all American. Available c/o Linda Magallon, 1083 Harvest Meadow Court, San Jose, CA 95136, USA.

Sundance. Published between 1976 and 1979, the six Sundance journals contain some excellent articles on dreams. The back copies can be obtained from Sundance, P.O. Box 595, Virginia Beach, VA 23451, USA.

General

Human Potential Resources. An extremely good directory of groups, courses and organisations. Appears every four months. Available from *Human Potential Magazine*, 5 Layton Road, London N1 0PX.

Self and Society. Publishes articles on Humanistic Psychology bi-monthly. Has also brought out two special editions on dreams (May/June 1981 and March/April 1983). Available from The Editor, *Self and Society*, 62 Southwark Bridge Road, London SE1.

Centres
London
Association for Self Help and Community Groups, 7 Chesham

Terrace, Ealing, London W13. Workshops for people who want to start their own self help groups, run by Hans Lobstein.

Institute of Psychosynthesis, 310 Finchley Road, London NW3.

Psychosynthesis and Education Trust, 188 Old Street, London EC1. Runs courses which include guided imagery and dreams.

Rochester Foundation, 8/9 Rochester Terrace, London NW1. Particular focus on Gestalt dreamwork.

Metanoia, 13 North Common Road, London W5 2QB. A psychotherapy Training Institute, with occasional dream groups.

Edinburgh
Wellspring, 13 Smiths Place, Edinburgh 6. Regular dream groups.

Combe Martin
Dream Research Centre, King Street, Combe Martin, Devon EX34 0A6. As well as supporting individuals and groups working with their dreams, the centre runs a dream interpretation service.

Bath
Openings, Bluecoat House, Saw Close, Bath BA1 1EY. A variety of groups including dream groups by difference facilitators.

Other Contacts

Manchester
Brenda Mallon, 20 Circular Road, Manchester 20. Particular interest in women's dreams.

Edinburgh
Hilary Scaife, 2 Old Farm Cottage, Quarryford, by Gifford, East Lothian EH41 4P1. Professional dreamwork training and workshops in the Jungian-Senoi process with Strephon Kaplan Williams and other staff.

REFERENCES

Chapter 1
1. Alan McGlashan, *Gravity and Levity* (Chatto and Windus, 1976) p. 92.

Chapter 2
1. Erich Fromm, *The Forgotten Language* (Grove Press 1951).
2. Alan McGlashan, *The Savage and Beautiful Country* (Chatto and Windus, 1970).
3. Jeremy Taylor, *Dream Work* (Paulist Press, 1983).
4. Ann Faraday, *Dream Power* (Berkely, 1972).
5. Erich Fromm, op cit, pp. 3-4
6. *Ibid*, p.33
7. *Ibid*, p.7
8. *Ibid*, pp.7-9
9. *Ibid*, pp.42-44
10. Calvin Hall, *The Individual and His Dreams* (Signet, 1972).

Chapter 3
1. William Dement, *Some Must Watch While Some Must Sleep* (Norton, 1972).
2. Ann Faraday, *The Dream Game* (Harper Row, 1976).
3. Ralph Woods and Herbert Greenhouse, *The New World of Dreams* (Macmillan, 1974) p.250.

4.   Erich Fromm, *The Forgotten Language* (Grove Press, 1951).
5.   Strephon Kaplan Williams, *The Dreamwork Manual* (The Aquarian Press, 1984).
6.   Calvin Hall, *The Individual and His Dreams* (Signet, 1972).
7.   Patricia Garfield, *Creative Dreaming* (Futura, 1974).
8.   James Hillman, *The Dream and the Underworld* (Harper and Row, 1979).
9.   Jeremy Taylor, *Dream Work* (Paulist Press, 1983).
10.   Ralph Woods and Herbert Greenhouse, *The New World of Dreams* (Macmillan, 1974).

Chapter 4
1.   From an interview with Laurens van der Post in *Parabola* Vol. Vii, No. 2.
2.   Strephon Kaplan Williams, *The Dreamwork Manual* (The Aquarian Press, 1984).

Chapter 5
1.   Strephon Kaplan Williams, *The Dreamwork Manual* (The Aquarian Press, 1984).
2.   Tony Crisp, *The Instant Dream Book* (Spearman, 1984).
3.   Strephon Williams, op. cit.
4.   Calvin Hall, *The Meaning of Dreams* (McGraw-Hill, 1966).
5.   Fritz Perls, *Gestalt Therapy Verbatim* (Real People Press, 1969).
6.   Gayle Delaney, *Living Your Dreams* (Harper Row, 1979).

Chapter 6
1.   Bernard Steinzor, *The Healing Partnership* (Harper Row, 1967).
2.   Richard Corriere, Werner Karle, Lee Woldenberg, Joseph Hart, *Dreaming and Waking* (Peace Press, 1980).
3.   Kilton Stewart, 'Dream Theory in Malaya', in C. Tart (ed) *Altered States of Consciousness* (John Wiley, 1969).
4.   Patricia Garfield, *Creative Dreaming* (Futura, 1974) p.103.
5.   Corriere *et al* op cit.
6.   *Ibid*, pp.103, 112.
7.   *Ibid*, pp.108-109.
8.   See in particular 'Dream Network Bulletin' (Vol. 3-4, March-April 1984) for an article by Ann Faraday and John Wren Lewis. This journal is available from 487 Fourth Street, Brooklyn, N.Y. 11215.
9.   Corriere *et al*, op. cit. pp.100-101.

10. *Ibid*, p.176
11. Bernard Steinzor, op cit.
12. Tony Crisp, *The Instant Dream Book* (Spearman, 1984).
13. *Self and Society*, Journal of Humanistic Psychology (May/June 1981). Article by Gaie Houston.

Chapter 7
1. Tony Crisp, *The Instant Dream Book* (Spearman, 1984).
2. Diane Mariechild, *Mother Wit* (Crossing Press, 1981).
3. Markowitz, Taylor and Bokert, 'Dream Discussion as a Means of Opening Blocked Familial Communication', *Psychother. Psychosom 16:* 348-356 (1968).
4. *Human Potential Resources*, December-February 1984.
5. *Self and Society*, March/April 1983. A special edition on dreams. A follow-up to the May/June 1981 issue mentioned above, also devoted to dreams.
6. *Dream Network Bulletin*, Vol.2, No.11 (November 1983).

Chapter 9
1. Monte Ullman, *Working with Dreams* (Hutchinson, 1983).
2. Moreno *Psychodrama. Action Therapy and Principles of Practice* Volume 3. pp.242-244 (Beacon House, 1969).

Chapter 10
1. Sheldon Kopp, *If You Meet The Buddha on the Road, Kill Him* (Sheldon Press, 1974), p.15.
2. Sheila Ernst and Lucy Goodison, *In Our Own Hands* (Women's Press, 1981).
3. For a very readable account of group dynamics see Wiliam Schutz, *Elements of Encounter* (Joy Press, 1973). Slightly more technical is Bion, W. R., *Experiences in Groups* (Tavistock, 1961).

Chapter 11
1. Sheldon Kopp, *If You Meet The Buddha on the Road, Kill Him* (Sheldon Press, 1974), p.15.

INDEX